TOO CLOSE FOR COMFORT

COPING WITH A DEPENDENT LOVED ONE

FOREWORD BY HOWIE MANDEL

TAMIR S. ALDAD, MD

Too Close for Comfort: *Coping with a Dependent Loved One*

MANHATTAN
BOOK GROUP

Published by Manhattan Book Group
447 Broadway 2nd Floor, #354, New York, NY 10013
(212) 634-7677 | www.manhattanbookgroup.com

Printed in the United States of America
ISBN-13: 978-1-970844-96-2

CONTENTS

DEDICATION

For my wife, Shiran, whose strength, independence, and trust give me the freedom to think, build, and grow. Her support has never been conditional, and her love has always made space rather than demanded it.

And for our four children whom I love deeply. I want you to know that no one is immune to dependency, and no one is above needing care. Anyone can lean too hard, and anyone can become the one others lean on. My hope is that this book helps you move through relationships with awareness, integrity, and the confidence to love without losing yourselves.

And for my parents and brothers, thank you for believing in me on the days I questioned myself. Your faith carried me further than you know.

FOREWORD BY HOWIE MANDEL

I've spent most of my life talking about what's going on inside my head.

If you've followed me for any amount of time, you know I've been open about my struggles with OCD and anxiety. I've talked about the intrusive thoughts, the need for control, the rituals that don't always make sense to anyone else but feel necessary to me. For a long time, just saying those things out loud felt like progress. And in many ways, it was.

But there's another side to that story that I didn't fully understand until much later.

Mental health doesn't exist in isolation. It doesn't just live inside one person. It shows up in relationships. It shapes conversations, routines, expectations, and sometimes even the roles people take on without realizing it. The truth is, when one person is struggling, the people around them often begin to adjust in ways that are subtle at first and then, over time, become part of the fabric of everyday life.

Not because they're weak. Not because they're doing anything wrong. But because they care.

Looking back, I can see how the people closest to me learned to navigate my world alongside me. There's a kind of quiet strength in that. A willingness to adapt. To support. To make things work. And while that kind of love is incredibly powerful, it can also be complicated.

That's where this book comes in.

Dr. Tamir Aldad takes a perspective that we don't talk about nearly enough. We spend a lot of time trying to understand the person who is struggling. We talk about diagnoses, symptoms, treatment plans. But we don't spend nearly enough time talking about the people who are standing right next to them, doing their best to help, often without a clear roadmap.

What I appreciate about this book is that it doesn't point fingers. It doesn't assign blame. Instead, it shines a light on patterns that are incredibly common and yet rarely named. It helps explain why well-intentioned support can sometimes turn into something heavier. Something that feels less like helping and more like carrying.

And more importantly, it offers a way forward.

If you've ever found yourself adjusting your life around someone you love, trying to keep the peace, trying to make things easier, trying to do the right thing without being entirely sure what that is, you'll see yourself in these pages. And you'll likely feel something even more important: understood.

This book isn't about stepping away from people. It's about learning how to show up in a way that's healthier, clearer, and ultimately more sustainable for everyone involved.

I've had the privilege of sharing my story publicly, and I know how powerful it can be to put words to something that feels hard to explain. What Dr. Aldad has done here is give language to a different side of that experience. One that matters just as much.

Because mental health isn't just about what happens inside a person.

It's about what happens between people.

And understanding that might be one of the most important steps forward we can take.

— Howie Mandel

INTRODUCTION

A Direct Word to the Reader

If you are holding this book, there is a good chance you are tired in a way that is hard to explain.

Not the kind of tired that sleep fixes. Not the tiredness of a busy season or a demanding job. This is a deeper exhaustion that comes from caring constantly, thinking constantly, anticipating constantly, and still feeling as though it is never quite enough.

You may be someone who loves deeply. Someone others rely on. Someone who shows up. And yet, somewhere along the way, caring began to cost more than it should. You started to feel anxious when things were calm, guilty when you rested, and responsible for emotions and outcomes that were never fully yours to manage. You may have wondered whether this is simply what love requires, or whether something has quietly gone wrong.

This book is not here to tell you to walk away, harden yourself, or stop caring. It is not here to label people as toxic or reduce complex relationships to slogans. And it is not here to convince you that choosing yourself means abandoning others. It is here to offer something more precise.

This book is about what happens when care turns into over-responsibility. When love becomes fused with urgency. When guilt masquerades as morality. When being a good partner, parent, child, or leader requires you to slowly disappear.

Many people reach for words like "codependency" or "burnout" to describe this experience, but those labels often fail to capture the internal confusion. You may know something feels off, but still feel selfish for naming it. You may sense the way you care is unsustainable but fear that changing would make you cruel.

If any of this resonates, you are not weak, broken, or incapable of love. You are likely operating under a model of caring that was never meant to be carried indefinitely.

The purpose of this book is not to take care away from you. It is to give it back to you in a form that does not require self-erasure. To help you distinguish love from obligation, compassion from control, and responsibility from rescue. To show you how to care in a way that is steady, dignified, and sustainable for you and for the people you love.

You do not need to have answers yet. You do not need to know whether you will stay, leave, or renegotiate the relationships in your life. You only need a willingness to look honestly at what caring has come to mean for you—and what it has been costing.

Why This Question Became Personal

I did not come to this work because I was always good at boundaries.

I first encountered the cost of blurred power and emotional invalidation in middle school. During those years, I spent prolonged time in environments where my experience was repeatedly dismissed or reframed by peers and authority figures alike. When conflict arose, I was often cast as the problem, even when my perspective was never fully explored or taken seriously.

What made that period particularly damaging was not any single event, but the chronic nature of it. I had no clear advocate, no reliable containment, and no meaningful exit. Over time, that kind of exposure teaches a nervous system to adapt rather than resist. You learn to anticipate reactions, minimize yourself, and endure quietly. You learn that peace is achieved not through fairness but through compliance.

In environments like that, survival strategies develop quickly. You become vigilant. You scan the emotional weather. You learn how to absorb discomfort without complaint. These adaptations are not signs of weakness. They are signs of intelligence under pressure. But they come with a cost. They teach the body that safety depends on self-suppression and that speaking up may only make things worse.

There was a point during that period of my life when the sense of being trapped became dangerous to my own thinking. That moment forced clarity. Something about the structure of my environment was not only unhealthy but unsustainable.

High school marked a shift.

With distance from that earlier setting, I began to recognize the importance of boundaries, agency, and self-definition. I learned that not every environment deserves your endurance and that growth sometimes requires separation. I became more intentional about the relationships I entered and more attentive to the subtle ways dependency can form on either side of a dynamic.

This was not about erasing what came before but rather about integrating and learning from my past. The earlier experience sharpened my awareness of power, responsibility, and emotional safety. The growth that followed taught me that care does not require collapse. Resilience is not the same as endurance.

I share this not to center my past or assign blame where it does not belong. My family was not the source of this invalidation, nor were they absent from my growth. This distinction matters. The experiences that shaped my sensitivity to these dynamics occurred in specific institutional and peer environments, not within my home.

I include this context for one reason: it shaped the lens through which I later came to see similar patterns in others. It taught me how easily good people adapt to unhealthy systems, how quietly responsibility shifts, and how difficult it can be to recognize when survival strategies have outlived their usefulness.

That awareness followed me into my professional life where the same structures appeared again and again in different forms.

From Experience to Psychiatry

I did not enter psychiatry to explain my past. I entered it to understand patterns I kept seeing long after that difficult chapter of my life closed.

As I moved into adulthood, one question stayed with me: why do some people remain whole under pressure while others slowly disappear in the act of caring? Why do intelligent, capable people end up organizing their lives around managing someone else's emotions, crises, or instability, even when it is clearly costing them their health, relationships, and sense of self?

That question led me to psychiatry and later to addiction psychiatry. Addiction work forces you to confront dependency in its most distilled form. You see how quickly concern turns into control, how easily love slides into rescue, and how often well-intentioned caretaking unintentionally reinforces the very problems it is trying to solve. You also see how frequently guilt, fear, and responsibility are misassigned. Not because people are naïve, but because they have been taught that good care requires constant intervention.

During residency and fellowship, I began to notice something that often went unnamed. Many of the people suffering the most were not the ones using substances or acting out. They were the partners, parents, adult children, colleagues, and leaders who had quietly taken on the role of stabilizer. They were exhausted, vigilant, morally conflicted, and deeply confused about where their responsibility ended.

They would say things like, "I can't step back, or they'll fall apart," or, "If I don't stay on top of this, something bad will happen."

Clinically, these individuals often presented with anxiety, depression, burnout, insomnia, or a vague sense of emptiness. But underneath the symptoms was a common structure. Their nervous systems were organized around prevention. Their sense of worth had become fused with being needed. Their version of care required constant vigilance rather than presence.

As my career progressed, this pattern became impossible to ignore. I saw it not only in addiction settings, but across mental healthcare more broadly. In couples work. In family systems. In high-functioning professionals. In leaders who carried entire organizations emotionally not just operationally.

Today, as a board-certified psychiatrist and the CEO of a mental health urgent care organization serving patients nationally, I see these dynamics at scale. Through different diagnoses, demographics, and life circumstances, these structures remain strikingly consistent. Good people over-carrying what was never meant to be theirs.

And not for lack of insight or intention. Usually, they lacked a good model growing up. Most people were never taught how to care without overfunctioning, how to love without rescuing, or how to tolerate someone else's distress without seeing it as an emergency or moral failure.

This book grew out of that realization.

My goal is not to make people care less. Instead, it is an attempt to help people care more accurately.

What I've Seen, Repeatedly

Once you begin looking for this pattern, it becomes difficult to stop seeing it everywhere.

It appears across diagnoses, life stages, and relationship types. In people who are outwardly successful but inwardly exhausted. In those who pride themselves on being reliable, strong, and emotionally intelligent, but still find themselves quietly reorganizing their lives around someone else's distress.

In clinical settings, these individuals often arrive with secondary complaints. Anxiety that will not settle. Sleep that never feels restorative. Burnout that does not improve with time off. Depression without a clear cause. A persistent sense of being trapped even in relationships they care deeply about.

Many say some version of, "Nothing is technically wrong, but I feel like I'm disappearing." Others frame their suffering as a personal failure. What they rarely see is that their nervous systems have been placed in a chronic state of responsibility that no amount of insight or willpower can sustain.

I have often seen this pattern in the partners of people with addiction, where concern turns into monitoring and prevention at the cost of one's own well-being. I have seen it in adult children of emotionally dependent parents where guilt masquerades as love and separation feels like betrayal. I have seen it in high-performing professionals who carry teams, families, and relationships emotionally—not because they are asked to, but because they do not know how to do anything else.

In leadership roles, the pattern can be even harder to spot. Absorbing stress is mistaken for strength. Emotional labor is performed invisibly. Burnout is reframed as weakness rather than recognized as a signal that responsibility has been misallocated.

Across settings, the details change, but the structure does not.

Care becomes fused with urgency.

Responsibility expands beyond its rightful boundaries.

Guilt becomes a governing force rather than a moral signal.

Calm is chased, not cultivated.

This pattern is particularly hard to identify and address because these behaviors are often praised. People are described as loyal, compassionate, indispensable. The system relies on their overfunctioning, and the cycle reinforces itself.

Individuals' suffering rarely announces itself dramatically. Instead, life narrows. There is less spontaneity and joy. More vigilance and mental rehearsal. More emotional labor performed in silence.

When many people finally seek help, they are not asking how to change the relationship. They are asking how to endure it.

This is where traditional advice often fails. Boundaries without guilt work do not hold. Self-care without responsibility reassignment feels hollow. Insight without a new internal model leaves people stuck.

People suffering from dependency do not lack compassion or effort. What they need is a new framework for healthy relationships. A way to understand where care ends and carrying begins and an understanding of why that distinction matters at a nervous system level.

This book is an attempt to name that distinction clearly.

Naming the Core Problem

At the center of most suffocating relationships is a confusion about responsibility.

Caring for someone and carrying someone are not the same thing, though they often feel indistinguishable from inside the relationship.

Caring means emotional investment without ownership. You notice. You feel concern. You respond when appropriate. You remain connected without taking responsibility for outcomes that are not yours.

Unhealthy carrying begins when that responsibility shifts. You start to feel accountable for how the other person feels, behaves, or copes. Their distress becomes your emergency. Their instability becomes your problem to solve. Calm becomes something you must produce.

This shift happens gradually. You step in "just this once." You smooth things over. You prevent a blow-up. Each intervention brings short-term relief, reinforcing your belief that this is what a caring relationship requires.

Over time, your nervous system learns a dangerous equation: if they are okay, I am okay.

Guilt keeps the system running. Dependency grows, not because anyone intends it to, but because responsibility in the relationship has been misassigned.

This way of being in a relationship fails everyone involved.

The person who carries becomes exhausted and disconnected from themselves. The person being carried is denied the opportunity to build agency and tolerance. And because moments of calm occur, a broken system is mistaken for a successful one.

This book challenges the assumption that creating boundaries and stepping back means abandoning love. Instead, it proposes that the problem is not that you care too much but that you have been taught a version of care that requires self-erasure. You do not need to care less. But you must learn to care in a way that is sustainable.

What This Book Will and Will Not Do

This book will not tell you to leave your relationship. It will not encourage emotional detachment or self-protective cruelty. It will not ask you to endure what is quietly destroying you in the name of loyalty or love.

It will help you slow down when guilt spikes, urgency rises, and responsibility blurs. It will help you understand what is happening in your nervous system, so you can respond with clarity rather than reflex.

There are no rigid rules here. This work is not about compliance. I aim to teach you to learn to interpret guilt correctly, tolerate discomfort, and return responsibility to its proper place.

You will not be rushed. There is no timeline for deciding whether to stay, leave, or renegotiate. Insight often needs time to settle in the body before it becomes action.

Above all, this book assumes you are capable of care that is both compassionate and boundaried even if you have never been shown how to hold those two things together.

A Steady Invitation

If there is one thing to know before you begin, it is this: you do not need to become someone else to do this work. You will not have to learn to care less to have healthy relationships.

Still, it may not be an easy read. If guilt rises as you read, pause. If urgency tightens, pause. Those moments are not failures. They are information.

You are not alone in this experience. These patterns are common and changeable. With clarity and patience, care can become something that nourishes without draining you, that connects but does not consume you.

We will take this step by step. Thoughtfully and without forcing outcomes. With respect for both your limits and your humanity.

When you are ready, turn the page.

CHAPTER 1

When Love Feels Like a Cage

I am a psychiatrist who treats addiction and complex mental health conditions, and I lead a mental health urgent care system where I see people at their breaking point every day. But the people I want to talk to first in this book are not the ones in crisis themselves.

They are the ones who quietly rearranged their lives to keep someone else steady.

They are the ones who cancelled plans again. Skipped the gym. Passed on dinner with friends. Put their own needs on hold, not because they wanted to, but because it felt easier than dealing with the fallout of not doing it.

That moment is usually small. Ordinary. Easy to justify.

You were going to go work out, but they were overwhelmed.

You had plans, but they were anxious.

You needed quiet, but they needed reassurance.

So you adjusted. Again.

Not because you are weak or don't value yourself. But because you care, and because the conflict feels worse than the inconvenience.

The quiet trade you keep making

Most people in this position would never describe their relationship as unhealthy. They describe it as *hard*. Or *complicated*. Or *just a lot right now*.

They say things like, "It isn't easy, but they have no one else, and they need me."

That sentence tells me everything.

It tells me you have placed yourself last without realizing you did it. It tells me you have accepted a level of responsibility that no one person can carry indefinitely. And it tells me you are already tired even if you haven't fully admitted it yet.

This dynamic can be so confusing because the sacrifices feel moral. They feel like the loving choice—like what a good partner, child, or parent would do.

You tell yourself:

> "This is what anyone else would do in my position."
>
> "They would do this for me too if I really needed them."
>
> "Maybe I'm just stressed and making this a bigger deal than it really is."

These thoughts are not irrational, but they are insidious. These patterns of thinking explain how people stay in situations that slowly erase and drain them.

When caring starts to cost you

At first, the cost is subtle. You rationalize it.

You tell yourself it's normal to feel a little drained. That everyone puts their needs second sometimes. That relationships require compromise.

But what I see, over and over, is that it's not someone's energy that disappears first. It's their autonomy.

You stop choosing freely. You start calculating.

Will this upset them?

Will this trigger anxiety?

Will it be easier to just handle it myself?

Your priorities blur. Your identity softens at the edges. Your quiet time, the time you need to reset and recharge, becomes negotiable. You promise yourself you'll get back to it once things calm down, but they don't.

Instead, a strange emotional pattern sets in. You only feel relief when they feel calm. When they feel distressed, your body tightens. Your nervous system stays on alert even during moments that should be yours.

You may not realize how much of your mental space they occupy until you imagine what it would feel like not to be on call. Yet, that thought alone can make you uncomfortable.

The question you don't want to ask

At some point, usually late at night or in a quiet moment, a question surfaces that you push away as quickly as it appears.

"Is this really what love is supposed to feel like?"

The question scares you. It feels disloyal, ungrateful, or harsh. You tell yourself you shouldn't be thinking this way. That other people have it worse. That you should be more patient, more understanding, more generous. You bury the question.

But it keeps coming back because your body knows something your brain is trying to override. Love should not feel like a cage.

Naming the problem: Why this book exists

The person you love is not bad, broken, or intentionally hurting you. And you have not failed or done anything wrong.

But you may be in a relationship that is not healthy for you, a relationship that is built on a pattern that leaves one person slowly disappearing while the other cannot function alone.

You are not cruel for wanting your life to feel like your own again, and you are not selfish for wanting—**or even needing**—to put yourself first sometimes.

In the chapters ahead, I will give you a clear framework for understanding the dynamics of codependence, identifying this pattern of behavior, and ultimately learning a new way to be in relationship with others.

For now, I want you to hold onto one thing.

If love has started to feel like obligation, if care has turned into constant sacrifice, and if your world has grown smaller while someone else's fear has grown louder, you are not alone. And you can learn to live differently.

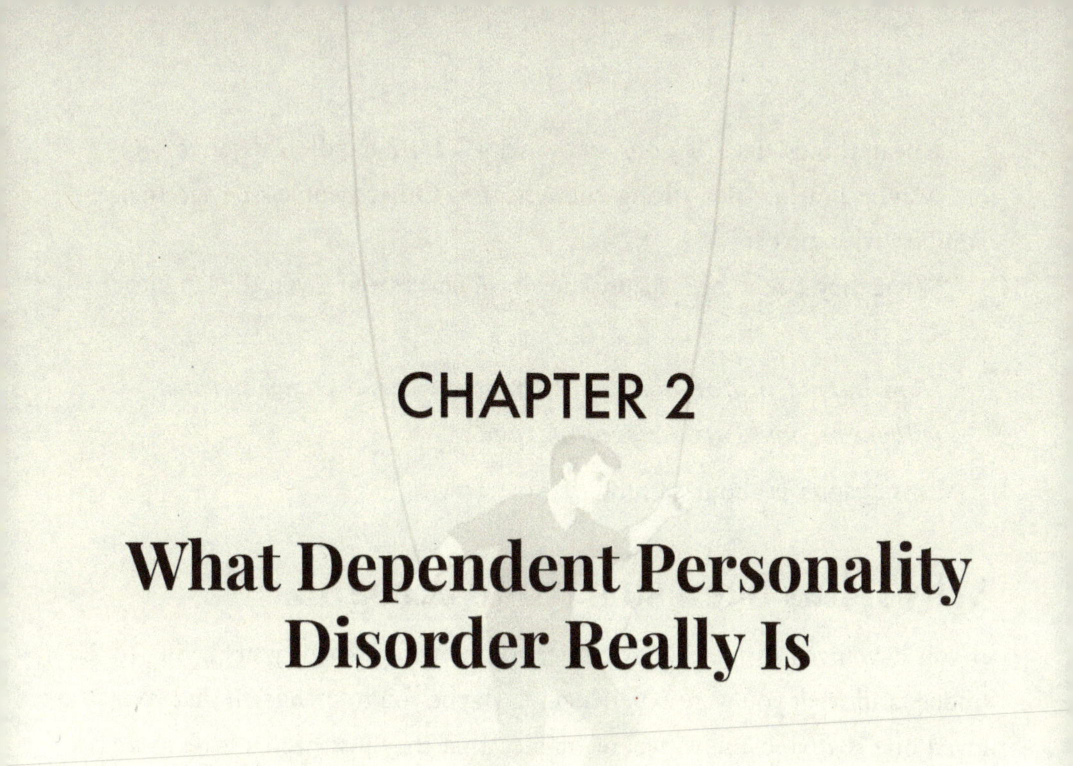

CHAPTER 2

What Dependent Personality Disorder Really Is

In mental health urgent care, I do not just treat anxiety, depression, or addiction. I treat the people who have been carrying everyone else for too long.

They come in exhausted, guilty, and confused. On paper, many of them look high-functioning. They hold jobs. They show up for their families. It's likely everyone calls them the reliable one. Maybe they're the person everyone calls when something goes wrong. But for them, something is breaking underneath.

Often these patients do not come in complaining about boundary or relationship issues. Maybe they cannot sleep, or their anxiety has become unbearable. Some are seeking help because they started drinking or using substances in a way that scares them. When I ask what led them to therapy, the story is often not about chaos or recklessness. It is about obligation and being needed. It's about being leaned on so heavily that there is no room left to breathe.

I hear things like, "I don't know why I can't handle this anymore," or "Maybe I'm just not strong enough," or "Other people manage their families, why can't I?"

What they rarely say, because they have never been given the language for it, is this:

I am trapped in a relationship where someone else cannot function without me, and I am disappearing inside it.

This chapter is about naming that pattern.

Why it has been so hard to recognize

If you have lived inside this dynamic, you may have spent years trying to understand what you were experiencing. Maybe you told yourself that your loved one is anxious, sensitive, or fragile. That they just need a little more support right now. Maybe you wondered whether this is simply what love looks like. What it means to be a good partner, child, or parent.

Popular psychology has not helped. Much of the language available focuses on codependency, attachment styles, and people pleasing. Those frameworks can be useful in some contexts, but in this one, they can miss the mark.

In many of the families I see, the two people are not equally entangled. It is not a mutual dance of dysfunction but a one-way transfer of responsibility. One person increasingly cannot tolerate being alone with decisions, uncertainty, or distress. The other becomes the regulator and stabilizer. Caring has been quietly redefined as carrying.

What Dependent Personality Disorder looks like from the outside

Dependent Personality Disorder is a real and under-recognized diagnosis. But as the loved one, the name matters less than the experience.

From the outside, the pattern often looks like this:

> Decisions slowly migrate to you. What should I say. What should I do. Can you check this. Can you handle this. Can you be here. Can you fix this.
>
> Reassurance never lasts. You answer the question, calm the fear, solve the problem. Relief comes but only briefly. Then the next wave hits. Sometimes minutes later. Sometimes the next day.
>
> Independence does not bring pride. It brings panic. When you encourage the other person's autonomy, it is not received as support. It is felt as abandonment.

Your life shrinks around their needs. Your schedule. Your work. Your friendships. Your gym. Your rest. Everything becomes negotiable except their needs and their distress.

You begin to feel resentful, then guilty for feeling resentful. You start apologizing for needing space. You tell half-truths to avoid triggering anxiety. You carry the weight quietly because it feels cruel not to.

If any of this sounds familiar, you are not failing at love. You are inside a system that places an unfair burden of regulation on you.

What is happening inside the person you love

It is important to say this clearly. People with Dependent Personality Disorder are not weak, lazy, or malicious. Most are deeply afraid.

For someone with strong dependent traits, being alone with uncertainty does not merely feel uncomfortable. It feels unsafe. Making decisions on their own can trigger real fear. Separation or alone time triggers panic. Eventually, any autonomy feels like being dropped without a net.

Their nervous system is not calibrated to tolerate distress independently, so it looks outward in search of a stabilizer. Over time, you may have become that stabilizer.

Your involvement in a situation can soothe their anxiety. Fast. When you reassure them, their internal alarm quiets. When you take over, their fear recedes. Over time, they become conditioned to expect and ultimately feel they need your involvement and support. Their brain learns, without intention or awareness, that safety lives outside themselves.

And your brain learns something too.

You learn that intervening works. And rescuing reduces distress. That stepping back leads to escalation. Over time, both nervous systems are trained. One to depend. The other to carry.

Why codependency language often gets this wrong

In addiction treatment, the term codependency has a specific history. It was meant to describe dynamics where people organize their lives around someone else's substance use in ways that perpetuate harm.

When that language is applied indiscriminately to relationships like this one, it is not always accurate and can even do damage.

Sometimes the framework of codependency places responsibility on the helper without acknowledging the imbalance that exists in the relationship. It can suggest mutual pathology where it does not exist. The codependency framework can imply that if you would only stop enabling, the problems would resolve.

In my experience, the codependency framework doesn't tell the full story in relationships characterized by a dependent personality.

I see one person whose ability to function has eroded, and another whose sense of obligation has been stretched beyond anything reasonable.

I see roles that have been quietly shifted. The partner becomes parent, the child becomes caretaker, and support becomes obligation.

When I explain this to loved ones, many are relieved and terrified at the same time. Relieved to understand why their current relationship feels unbearable. Still, they are often terrified that change means hurting someone they love, and this fear keeps the system intact.

The cost of staying as you are

Over time, this dependent dynamic extracts a price. Sometimes the cost is subtle at first with fatigue, irritability, and a constant low-grade tension. But, the consequences can be more severe with symptoms like burnout, depression, anxiety, or problematic substance use.

I have treated many people who turned to alcohol or other substances, not because they wanted to escape responsibility, but because they needed a moment where the weight lifted. Substance use gave them a moment where they could numb the pressure and regroup before going back to being of service.

Understanding Dependent Personality Disorder

Dependent Personality Disorder is a real but underrecognized diagnosis. Understanding this disorder and the relationship dynamics that it creates can be invaluable for people trying to maintain relationships with those who have this diagnosis.

Understanding the system you are trapped in can help you learn how to change it.

In the chapters ahead, we will talk about how to recognize and change this dynamic in a kind, boundaried manner. How to learn to set limits without feeling like you are doing something wrong or abandoning your partner. You can learn to step out of a role you never consciously agreed to play. What you are living with is real, difficult, but most importantly—fixable.

CHAPTER 3

Why They Can't Let Go

If you have ever wondered why independence seems to make things worse instead of better, this chapter is for you.

By now, you may understand that something has gone wrong in your relationship. Maybe you've started to recognize a pattern of dependency in your own life. You may even know that continuing this way is costing you more than you can afford. And yet, when you try to step back, set boundaries, or to say no, something snaps you right back into old patterns.

That something is fear and guilt.

This chapter will explain why grief and fear are so powerful, why insight alone has not been enough, and why love without boundaries quietly turns into something unhealthy for everyone.

Why autonomy feels dangerous to them

When I explain this dynamic to loved ones in real life, I do not start with psychological jargon, diagnoses, or criteria. I start with attachment and safety.

Early attachment teaches a child one of two basic lessons. Either closeness is safe and stable, or closeness is something you have to cling to in order to survive. When early experiences are inconsistent, overwhelming, or fragile, a child does not fully develop the ability to calm themselves from the inside. Their sense of safety never becomes internal. Instead, it lives in other people.

As an adult, that person may look capable in many ways—intelligent, independent, successful. But when they are alone with uncertainty, decision-making, or emotional distress, their system collapses. On their own, negative emotions feel intolerable and unmanageable. For someone struggling in this way, autonomy is scary. Independence does not make them feel empowered or strong. Typically, it triggers feelings of danger, rejection, and abandonment.

Reassurance then becomes a necessity, not a pleasure or comfort. Generally, people with these kinds of issues are very conflict-averse as avoiding disagreement has become a survival strategy. Staying in an unhealthy relationship might feel safer than risking being alone. And the expectations they place on a partner can be unreasonable and incredibly difficult to shoulder.

Why reassurance keeps getting louder, not quieter

When you step in, their anxiety drops. Quickly. When you answer the question, make the call, double-check the decision, or simply stay close, the internal alarm quiets.

Over time, your brain learns something too. You learn that intervening works and helping reduces distress, while stepping back leads to escalation. Eventually, one nervous system is trained to depend while the other learns to carry.

This is your reassurance, which only ever offers temporary relief for your dependent partner.

By placing too much responsibility on others, the dependent partner fails to learn independence. Instead of slowly learning to cope more effectively on their own, they learn to lean more on others—on you.

These learned patterns of behavior can be hard to undo. Understanding is the first step, but it's often not sufficient on its own. Unlearning takes real work.

Why the origin story is not the point

At this stage, many books would spend pages tracing this dynamic back to childhood, trauma, or temperament. There is a place for that work, but this book is not that place.

You are not anyone's psychiatrist. You are not responsible for how they got here or even for helping them understand how they got here. Your responsibility is to yourself. Your life is shrinking now, and it's your job to stop and reverse that process. The origin is less important than the loop you are living in today.

Understanding how a problematic behavioral pattern started can create empathy, but it does not change the behavior.

Why guilt becomes the leash

If fear keeps them attached to you, it's guilt that keeps you attached to them.

Guilt shows up the moment you consider placing a boundary. Setting even a small, simple limit might feel like cruelty. You worry you are being selfish. Are you abandoning someone who needs you?

So you soften and step back in. Once again, you become their hero. The unhealthy system remains intact.

This is the moment that frustrates me most as a clinician because it is where progress is lost.

Guilt is a powerful opponent and a major inhibitor to real behavioral change. Boundaries often collapse in the face of intense feelings of guilt.

Though everyone may agree that something is wrong, nothing changes. The short-term relief of avoiding guilty feelings seems easier than the long-term work of real change.

Here is the truth that is hard to hear and necessary to say.

Feelings of guilt in these relationships are often a sign that you are finally doing something different and right. It is not a sign that you're doing something wrong or being selfish. Guilt is a painful emotion, but it is often the cost of changing a system that's harming you.

Sometimes what's necessary is uncomfortable. If you never required your child to brush their teeth, they might love you in the moment, but they would not thank you later when left with cavities and pain. Dodging discomfort is not kindness. It's simply avoidance.

You have to decide whether you are seeking short-term peace or long-term healing. You cannot have both.

Fear explains behavior. It does not justify overreach.

It is important to say this clearly.

Fear explains why the dependent person reaches for you, but it does not justify controlling your time, consuming your energy, or expecting you to organize your life around their distress.

You can hold compassion without surrendering your life.

Understanding their fear does not have to mean you allow it to dictate your choices.

The role of secondary gains, named honestly

There is another piece of this dynamic that often goes unspoken. Secondary gains.

When someone consistently relies on you, certain things happen automatically. They avoid responsibility. They outsource distress. They reduce exposure to failure. They gain comfort and stability without having to tolerate the discomfort that can come with growth.

Most of this is subconscious. Many dependent individuals are not aware they are overly reliant on others or are offloading difficult work that should be theirs. They are not consciously plotting to avoid responsibility. They are regulating uncomfortable emotions the only way they know how. Naming secondary gains is not about apportioning blame or bad intent.

As long as the relationship structure allows and rewards dependence, dependence will continue. As long as guilt keeps you enmeshed, the system will stay intact.

You did not create this unhealthy dynamic. But your lack of action may be maintaining it.

Why insight alone has not been enough

By now, you may understand the dependent dynamic intellectually. And yet, when the moment comes to behave differently, to break the pattern, you still feel pulled back in.

You're not weak. The nervous system does not change through intellectual understanding alone.

Fear does not respond to logic. Guilt does not dissolve because you are right. Doing more of the same, even with better intentions, will keep producing the same outcome. These feelings will only dissipate when the relationship structure that you are embedded in changes.

What you are living with is not sustainable. And it will not resolve by trying harder, explaining better, or caring more.

In the next chapter, we will name the exact loop that keeps pulling both of you back into the same roles. You will learn to see it clearly, and more importantly, to finally interrupt it. Fear explains why this started. Limits are how it ends.

CHAPTER 4

The Cycle of Suffocation

Jason woke up before his alarm, already tense. The apartment was quiet, but his mind was not. A part of him listened for the first vibration of his phone, the morning check-in that always came before he brushed his teeth. Two minutes later, it buzzed on the nightstand.

Are you up?

I did not sleep

I think I messed up with my manager

Please look

I don't know what to do without you

Jason exhaled. He typed, I am here, then stopped. He could already see the next hour. Calm her. Open the laptop. Read the email. Fix the sentence. Offer a script for what to say. Promise to text before his first meeting. Promise to check again at lunch. Promise to call on the drive home.

By noon, he would feel a small wave of relief. She calmed down. The fire was out. He did it. Two hours later, the next flare would arrive. A question she had asked last week. A fear he had soothed yesterday. A new reason she could not take the next step without him. Relief would turn into a quiet ache. The ache would grow into resentment by evening. By night, guilt would drown the resentment. He would lie in bed and tell himself that she was trying, that he was strong, and that love means showing up. He would fall asleep tired and hopeful. Morning would come. The phone would buzz again.

This is the cycle. If you live with someone who leans on you for every decision, every reassurance, every next move, you already know it in your bones. There is a beginning, a middle, and an end, and none of it truly ends. It loops. It resets. It locks both of you in roles you never intended to play.

This chapter names that loop, explains why it is so sticky, and shows you the precise places where change is possible. When you see the cycle clearly, stop blaming yourself, and stop blaming him or her, you can start doing something different.

The Pattern You Feel But Cannot Name

Most readers recognize some version of the same sequence.

1. **Distress signal.** Your phone lights up. Your partner, parent, adult child, or colleague is overwhelmed, confused, or afraid. The message is urgent. The message is often vague. The feeling is, I cannot do this without you.

2. **Rescue response.** You move fast. You reassure. You solve. You shoulder the task. You provide the answer. You take the call. You spend the evening drafting the email or contacting the office or completing the form.

3. **Temporary relief.** They calm down. You calm down. The world feels orderly again. You tell yourself it was not that big of a deal. You tell yourself that anyone would help. For a moment, it feels good to be needed. It feels satisfying to be effective.

4. **Resentment creep.** The next morning, you feel a little lighter, but a thread of irritation remains. Your own tasks slipped. Your body is tense. You cannot remember the last night you were truly "off". You notice that gratitude, if it comes, fades fast.
5. **Guilt and reset.** The irritation makes you feel selfish. You tell yourself that you overreacted, that they cannot help it, that this is love. You soften. You reassure again. The system resets to Step 1.

The 4 R's

I call this the **Rescue**, **Relief**, **Resentment**, **Reset** loop. You may feel like the only person living inside it. You are not. The loop is common when one person has Dependent Personality Disorder, and it is also common in relationships that have strong dependency traits without a formal diagnosis.

The loop trains both people. It rewards the dependent person for seeking help, not for building skills. It rewards the helper for rescuing, not for setting limits. Both people learn fast. Both people suffer slowly.

Why the Cycle Is So Sticky

If the loop is miserable, why is it so hard to stop? It persists because it delivers short-term relief to both sides, and short-term relief is a powerful teacher.

- **For the dependent person,** help-seeking turns their internal siren down. Anxiety drops, sometimes from a nine to a two, within minutes. The brain learns - ask him or her and you will feel safe. The body learns - cling to the lifeline and danger passes. There is no malice here. There is conditioning.

- **For the helper,** rescuing solves two problems at once. It stops their distress, which reduces your distress. It also lets you feel competent. You become the architect of calm. You become the person who can hold everything together. There is no malice here either. There is relief, and a sense of control in a life that often feels unpredictable.

Relief is not the same as repair. Relief is a temporary painkiller but repair is real treatment. But the cycle favors painkillers.

There is also a belief system that reinforces the loop. Many helpers carry a private rule that sounds something like this, "Good people do not let loved ones suffer." Many dependent partners carry a private rule that sounds like this, "If I am alone, I will fail or be abandoned." Rules like these are powerful and invisible. They are often subconscious. But for people in enmeshed relationships, these rules can turn simple decisions into consequential moral tests.

Finally, there is the nervous system. If your loved one has DPD or strong dependency traits, independence will feel less like growth and more like danger to them. Expecting someone to act differently without new strategies for addressing that fear is like telling a person with a fear of flying to relax at takeoff. He or she is not being dramatic. Their body reads the situation as unsafe. To them, the safest thing, in that moment, is to reach for you.

How the Roles Slowly Change You

Many readers worry that they are becoming someone they do not recognize. You might notice these shifts.

- **Hypervigilance.** You scan for problems, draft answers in your head, rehearse how you will calm them next time. Even when nothing is wrong, you wait for the other shoe to drop. Your nervous system is on call.

- **Identity shrinkage.** Your day bends around their needs. Your preferences get quiet. Your plans are negotiated against their anxiety. You become a manager of moods more than a person with desires.
- **Selective honesty.** You tell partial truths to avoid panic. You say you have to work late, not because you must, but because you need an hour on your own. You reassure when you do not feel reassured yourself. You minimize your resentment to keep the peace.
- **Moral fatigue.** You cannot tell if you are loving or enabling. You do not know where kindness ends and self-erasure begins. You are tired of deciding.

Dependency changes the dependent person, and it also changes the one who keeps rescuing. It trains you to ignore your own limits. It teaches you to wear a calm face while you drown a little. The cycle does not stop because you are weak. It stops when you see it clearly and decide to practice something different.

A Clear Picture, So You Can Change It

Think of the loop as a simple diagram.

Trigger
A problem appears, real or anticipated. A text arrives. An assignment confuses him or her. A friend does not reply. He or she feels a threat.

Pull
He or she reaches for you. The request may look like confusion, fear, or even anger. The message is the same: I cannot do this alone.

Rescue
You respond. You reassure. You take the task. You handle the call. You take the wheel.

Relief
Anxiety drops for both of you. The crisis ends. Everyone can breathe.

Reinforcement
Both brains learn, do that again next time. The behavior gets stronger.

Hidden cost
Your resentment grows. His or her skills stall. The next trigger requires the same or more support. The loop tightens.

The picture is not meant to shame you. It is a map, and maps give you options. You can interrupt the loop at several places. You can also plan for the next loop because there will be one.

The Five Levers of Change

You do not have to fix everything at once. The cycle has five reliable levers. Pulling any one of them begins to change the system. Pulling more than one accelerates change.

Lever 1: Anticipate the trigger
Most partners can predict the top three situations that set the loop in motion. Work emails. Medical paperwork. Social plans. Begin there. Name them out loud when you are both calm. Agree on how the first ten minutes will go the next time they start to panic. Many loops are half a surprise and half a routine. Reduce the surprise.

Lever 2: Change the first message
The initial text or call is the spark. If you always respond within sixty seconds, try a ten-minute window when possible. If you always type the answer, try a brief validation plus a prompt: "I know this is hard, and you have handled similar things before. What is your first step?" Fast answers teach dependence. Slow, caring questions teach autonomy.

Lever 3: Do less, coach more

Rescuing solves the problem in front of you. Coaching solves the next five problems. Ask questions that restore agency: "What have you tried? What is one step you can take without me? What do you need to feel steady enough to take it?" If he or she truly cannot move, co-create a micro-step that they can execute, then step back again.

Lever 4: Install recovery time for yourself

You will not hold new boundaries if you are running on fumes. Schedule small, non-negotiable blocks that restore you, not because you deserve a treat, but because your nervous system must downshift to lead. Ten minutes of quiet after a rescue is not indulgent. It is maintenance. The next chapter will cover this in depth.

Lever 5: Pre-commit to a boundary

When both of you are calm, create a sentence you can repeat during the next loop. For example, I will help you think, but I will not take this over. Or I can review a draft at 7 pm, but not before. Pre-committed sentences lower guilt in the moment. You are not inventing a limit while someone is panicking. You are following a plan you both knew about.

Any one of these levers will feel awkward at first. That is normal. Awkward means you are not running the old program. The goal is not to be perfect. The goal is to be consistent enough that the loop loses some of its automatic power.

What About Real Crises

There are moments when stepping in fully is humane and necessary. Medical danger. Legal deadlines. Suicidal language. When safety is at stake, you protect safety first. The difference is what you do after the crisis ends.

When the fire is out, resist the drift back into the old routine. Name what happened. Agree on how you will plan for the next distressed moment. If every week feels like a fire, that is not a relationship problem you can solve alone. That is a clinical problem that needs professional help. Chapter 11 will show you what kind of help works and how to access it.

The Emotional Tolls You Can Stop Paying

The cycle extracts certain taxes. You may not notice them at first because they feel like the price of love. They are not. You can stop paying them.

- **The fake yes.** You say yes to requests that you want to refuse, then carry quiet anger. Practice the honest no, delivered with warmth. No, I cannot handle that tonight. I can talk it through with you for ten minutes now, and we can set a plan for tomorrow.
- **The collapse apology.** You apologize for having boundaries, or for having a life. Practice neutral statements without apology. I will turn my phone off between 10 pm and 7 am. If something urgent happens, call the neighbor, then call 911.
- **The secret scorecard.** You keep mental tallies of everything you do. They rarely add up to gratitude. Replace the scorecard with agreements. Agreements can be seen, kept, and measured. Resentment cannot.
- **The personal indictment.** You interpret every spike of their anxiety as a verdict on your worth or your kindness. It is not. His or her distress is a signal in their nervous system. You did not create it. You cannot carry it, and you are not cruel for refusing to carry it.

When you stop paying these taxes, you do not become cold. You become clear. Clarity is what allows kindness to hold its shape.

A Tale of Two Texts

Consider two versions of the same moment. In both, she texts Jason during a workday.

Old loop

She: I sent the email, I think it was wrong, I can't fix it, can you call them for me?

Jason: I will handle it, send me the contact, don't worry

She: thank you, I knew you would save this

Relief for both. Resentment by evening. Reset tomorrow.

New loop

She: I sent the email, I think it was wrong, I can't fix it, can you call them for me?

Jason: I know your stomach is in knots, you've fixed similar things before, what is one step you can take now?

She: I don't know! I am frozen! Seriously?

Jason: Write a two-sentence follow-up that clarifies your request. Send me that draft, I'll take a look at it at 5

She: Ugh, I will try

Relief comes slower. Dependence decreases. The next loop will be easier.

The difference is not a miracle. It is a script, a limit, and the tolerance to feel uncomfortable while you both practice.

Answering Common Objections

If I stop rescuing, they will fall apart.

In some moments, he or she will wobble. That does not mean you made a mistake. Wobbling is what happens when someone learns to ride a bike. You do not carry the bike to prevent wobbling. You steady the bike while he or she learns. If he or she tips dangerously, you intervene. Then you step back again.

It feels cruel to hold a line when he or she is scared.

Kindness without structure does not feel kind in the long run. It feels like quicksand. Structure is not cruel. Structure is scaffolding. It keeps both of you standing.

He or she says I am abandoning them.

Accusations are often attempts to pull the loop back into place. Respond to the fear without changing the plan. I hear that you feel alone. I am with you, and I am not taking this over.

Repetition retrains the nervous system, not debate. Actions are more important than words here.

What if they threaten to self-harm when I set limits

Take all threats seriously. Follow your crisis plan. Contact professionals if needed. After safety is secured, do not reward the threat by abandoning all limits forever. Work with a clinician to create a plan that protects safety and builds skills.

How This Chapter Connects to the Next

You cannot interrupt the loop without fuel in your own tank. Most helpers try to change the system while running on empty. That is like trying to fix a car on the highway at night without lights, without tools, and without gas. You can do it for a few minutes. You cannot do it for months.

Chapter 5 is about the oxygen mask concept. It is not a slogan. The need to take care of yourself first is a physiological reality. Your nervous system saturates, then it frays. When it frays, you default to old habits, including rescuing. When it is steady, you can tolerate discomfort long enough to establish a new pattern. You will learn how to refill your tank in ways that are practical, timed, and guilt-resistant.

A Closing Exercise, Seeing Your Own Loop

Take five minutes and sketch your last loop on a sheet of paper. Label each step: Trigger, Pull, Rescue, Relief, Reinforcement, Hidden cost. Write down one sentence you can say to yourself at each stage.

- **Trigger:** This is familiar. I am allowed to slow down.
- **Pull:** I can respond with warmth without taking over.
- **Rescue:** Coaching is help. Carrying is not always help.
- **Relief:** Relief is not repair. I will sit with uncomfortable feelings.
- **Reinforcement:** We will choose what to teach today.
- **Hidden cost:** My limits protect both of us over time.

Keep it on your phone or on your desk. You will forget every so often. That is fine. The point is not perfection. The point is practice. The loop formed through repetition, and it will unwind the same way.

Vignette, Revisited

The next morning, Jason's phone buzzed again. He watched it for a breath, then two. He picked it up and typed.

"I'm here. I know you're scared. Write the first two sentences you wish you had sent. I will review them at 5. You can handle the next step."

She wrote back, "I will try."

Jason put the phone down. His heart still raced a little. It would for a while. He stood up and made coffee. He opened his calendar and protected a block at lunch for a walk. He glanced at the sheet of paper on his desk with the six steps and the six sentences. He did not feel certain. He felt clear.

The loop had not disappeared. It had shifted a degree. That is how cycles end. Not with a single dramatic gesture, but with repeated small moves that teach every nervous system involved, we can do this differently.

Key Takeaways

- The **Rescue**, **Relief**, **Resentment**, **Reset** loop keeps both people stuck by rewarding short-term relief over long-term repair.
- The loop is powered by conditioning, private rules about love and safety, and nervous system reactions that make independence feel threatening.
- You can interrupt the loop at multiple points by anticipating triggers, slowing the first response, coaching instead of carrying, protecting your recovery time, and pre-committing to clear boundaries.
- Safety always comes first during true crises, then the work returns to skill building and structure.
- Progress looks like small shifts, held consistently. Clarity is kinder than constant rescue.

CHAPTER 5

Your Oxygen Mask First

Jason lay awake in the dark and listened to the apartment settle. The refrigerator hummed. A car door clicked somewhere on the street. In his chest, there was a tightness that did not let up. His phone was face down on the nightstand, silent for once, because he had put it on "do not disturb." He told himself it was just for thirty minutes. He told himself he would turn it back on soon.

He thought about the day. The sprint at work. The two missed workouts this week. The half lunch he ate at his desk. The way he said yes to a last-minute favor and heard his own voice sound cheerful when he knew he was out of gas. He thought about the three times his phone buzzed with panic, and the three times he jumped in. He thought about how proud he felt for keeping everything steady, and how that pride now sat next to something heavier that he did not want to name.

His phone did not buzz. He noticed that his mind did the buzzing for him. What if she needs me? What if she thinks I do not care? What if I am the selfish one? He turned the phone face up and watched the black screen like a sky that might flash with lightning. Thirty minutes passed. He did not turn it on.

He went to the kitchen and drank cold water and realized his hands were shaking. He looked at himself in the mirror and tried a sentence out loud, "I am not available for the next hour." The words felt strange. He tried again, slower. "I am not available for the next hour." This time, the words settled into his mouth like something he could survive saying.

This is where many helpers arrive just before change. Not at a grand climax. At a small threshold where the quiet truth shows up. You cannot keep running your nervous system in the red and expect it to behave like a calm guide. You cannot keep saying yes while your body is saying no and expect your voice to sound steady. You cannot keep carrying two lives and expect to remember your own.

You have to learn to **put your oxygen mask on first.** In a crisis on a plane, that sentence is a safety protocol. In your life, it is a biological and moral necessity. Without oxygen, your brain will pick speed over wisdom. Without oxygen, your boundaries will crumble. Without oxygen, you will rescue instead of coach, and you will call it love.

This chapter will make the instructions real. You will learn what "oxygen" means in your body and mind. You will learn why guilt is the enemy of regulation. You will learn a practical plan to steady your system in minutes and make it more resilient over weeks.

Why Your Brain Cannot Hold Boundaries When You Are Depleted

Most people try to set limits while running on fumes. Science explains why that fails.

1) **Sympathetic overdrive.**
When your stress system runs hot, your body pumps out adrenaline and cortisol. Heart rate edges up. Breath rides high in the chest. Peripheral vision narrows. In this state, your brain favors threat avoidance and short-term relief. Boundaries don't provide short-term relief, so they feel like threats. Instead of maintaining boundaries, you revert to old habits that will lower the threat level quickly, such as immediate reassurance or taking over the task.

2) **The prefrontal tax.**
The part of your brain that holds plans and values, the prefrontal cortex, is costly to run. Sleep debt, dehydration, and hunger lower its performance. When the prefrontal system is taxed, nuanced decisions get harder. Executive function and future planning become more difficult. It is easier to say yes now and pay later. It is easier to defer discomfort. With a taxed prefrontal cortex, it is hard to tolerate ten minutes of someone else's anxiety and even harder to tolerate your own.

3) **Learning favors relief.**
Generally, your brain wires itself around what reduces discomfort fastest. If rescuing creates immediate calm, your system will tag rescuing as a good move. If holding a boundary creates a spike of guilt, your system will tag boundaries as dangerous. You must teach your brain that brief discomfort is safe and that safe discomfort leads to better outcomes. That teaching requires you to feel steady enough to ride the wave of short-term negative emotion. It's hard to carry out your long-term values when your short-term systems

are screaming for air. For lasting change to happen, you have to put your oxygen mask on first.

The Moral Permission No One Gives You

Many helpers carry a private belief that sounds noble but is not realistic or sustainable. "Good people do not let loved ones suffer." The belief often expands into something even harsher. "If I take care of myself first, I am abandoning them." These beliefs turn taking care of yourself into a bad choice, a moral failing.

Here is a different truth. You cannot be a wall between someone you love and a tidal wave. You are a person in a boat with another person who is scared. If you refuse to bail water, both of you sink. If you bail water resentfully until your arms give out, both of you still sink, only later. If you keep your boat balanced and steady, you can teach the other person to paddle. You preserve both lives by refusing to drown.

You are responsible for the quality of help you give. You are not responsible for providing help at all hours, at all costs, in all forms. You are allowed to be unavailable. You are allowed to rest. You are allowed to want your own life to feel like a life.

Oxygen, Defined in Plain Terms

For our purposes, oxygen means two things.

- **Regulation** in the moment, enough to keep your voice calm, your breath even, and your prefrontal cortex online.
- **Restoration** across the day and week, enough to refill the basics that let you tolerate someone else's discomfort without collapsing or lashing out.

You do not need to run away, but you do need a reliable plan for taking care of yourself that you can run on hard days. Below is that plan, built for the real world.

The Two Minute Reset: Fast Oxygen When You Need It Now

Use this when your phone buzzes, your chest tightens, and you feel the tug to fix everything. It takes two minutes. Set a timer.

Step 1: Drop your shoulders for twenty seconds.
On the inhale, raise them toward your ears. On the exhale, let them fall. Repeat three times. This unlocks shoulder and neck tension that keeps your breathing shallow.

Step 2: Box breathe for one minute.
Inhale for four, hold for four, exhale for four, hold for four. Slow exhales flip your system toward parasympathetic tone. If holding feels stressful, skip the holds and extend the exhale to six.

Step 3: Say the anchor sentence.
Quietly say, "I can respond with care without taking over." You are reminding your brain that there is a third option between rescue and withdrawal.

Step 4: Choose your response window.
Pick a time to respond that is not right now. Two minutes. Ten minutes. Thirty minutes. Put the phone face down. Let your body feel the small victory of not sprinting.

Now respond from a steadier place. You will notice that your words are simpler and your limits are clearer.

The 5 Daily Minimums: What Your System Needs to Stay Steady

On any hard day, meet these minimums. They are small on purpose. Minimums remove drama. Minimums are doable.

1) **Water, two tall glasses before noon.**

Hydration lifts energy and attention. Keep a bottle on your desk and finish it twice before midday.

2) **Protein at breakfast.**

Stable blood sugar stabilizes mood and reduces midmorning reactivity. Aim for twenty grams or more. It does not need to be perfect. It needs to be present.

3) **One real break before 3 pm.**

Walk around the block. Sit quietly without your phone. Stretch your back against a wall. Ten minutes counts. Your nervous system needs a pressure valve during the day, not only at night.

4) **A plan for the evening phone.**

Pick one of these and follow it:

Option A - phone on do not disturb during dinner and for thirty minutes before bed.

Option B - leave the phone in another room and tell yourself exactly where it is.

Option C - set a rule that you only reply to non-urgent messages after a fifteen-minute delay.

5) **Boring Bedtime.**

Aim for a lights-out time and protect it three nights a week. Sleep debt accumulates fast and robs you of all your better skills. You cannot outthink exhaustion.

If you meet these five minimums on more days than not, you will notice that your tone changes, your patience lengthens, and your capacity to stay calm improves.

Your Weekly Refill: A Small Routine That Makes a Big Difference

Use the weekend to reset. Keep it simple.

1) **One longer movement session, forty-five to sixty minutes.**
Walk in a park. Lift weights. Take a class. Think of it as sweeping your nervous system clean. You are teaching your body that it can rev high in a safe way and then come back down.

2) **A 90-minute block with no favors and no phone.**
Read, cook, fix something, meet a friend, sit by water. The activity matters less than the rule. This time belongs to you.

3) **Five-minute audit and plan.**
Look back at the week. Where did you rescue because you were too depleted to maintain your boundaries? Decide one change for next week. Write it down as a sentence you can speak. Example, "I will review their email drafts at 7 pm, not during work hours."

Guilt Management, So Your Boundaries Survive

Even with a good plan, guilt will try to knock your oxygen mask off your face. Expect it and prepare for it.

Name the guilt precisely.
Is it fear of being seen as cruel? Fear of being replaced? Fear of being wrong? Naming it strips away the fog and gives you something you can answer directly. The guilty feelings may seem less reasonable—and thus easier to move past—if you're more precise about them.

Answer guilt with purpose, not debate.
Repeat a purpose sentence that fits your values. "I am holding this limit so both of us learn a new pattern." "I am choosing discomfort now to prevent exhaustion later." When guilt argues with you, hold onto your purpose

Borrow another person's eyes.
Imagine a friend sitting beside you. If they watched your day, would they call you selfish for resting, eating, pausing before responding, or turning off your phone at night? Almost always, the answer is no. Use that outside perspective to reset your own.

Use the five reply rule.
When guilt pushes you to overexplain a boundary, count your attempts. If you have explained it 4 times, stop. State the boundary one more time for a total of 5 times and move on. Over-explaining teaches your own nervous system that your boundary is weak.

Scripts That Protect You While Respecting Them

These short scripts are firm, warm, and repeatable. Use them as written or as templates.

When the panic first arrives
I see you are overwhelmed. I will check my phone at 5 pm and can review one draft then.

When you are being pulled to take over
I am here to think with you. I am not taking this over. What is your first step?

When you need to end a call
I have ten minutes now. Then I am off my phone until evening. Let us focus on the next action you can take.

When you hear an accusation

I hear that you feel alone. I am here, and I am keeping this limit. We can talk after dinner.

When the situation is not urgent but is intense

I care about this. It is not urgent. I will give it attention at 7 pm. Please send me a 2-sentence summary by then.

Notice the pattern here. You validate their feelings. Tell them your plan. You invite them to take a step on their own. You do not explain, defend, or justify the boundary. You hold it.

What About Real Emergencies

Safety comes first. If you hear suicidal language, medical danger, or situations that genuinely cannot wait, act. Use your crisis plan. Involve professionals. Make the call.

After the crisis, return to the plan. Say this clearly. "Last night was a crisis, so I stepped in fully. Tonight is not a crisis. We will go back to our plan." This simple sentence prevents the emergency from resetting the entire relationship to old habits.

If every week contains an emergency, this is not a relationship problem you can manage alone. It is a clinical situation that requires professional care. Chapter 11 will show you what works and how to find it.

The Boundary Endurance Curve

Most people can hold a new boundary for a few days. Then something shakes them. The other person pushes harder. The week gets busy. Sleep slips. You default to rescue and call it a failure, but it takes time to build new habits.

Think of your limits like a new muscle. At first, they fatigue quickly. With practice, they last longer. With recovery, they rebuild stronger. Your job is not to hold perfectly. Your job is to notice two things. How far you can go before you crumble, and what refills you fastest.

Use this small tracker for the next two weeks.

- Sleep last night: hours and quality
- Water by noon: yes or no
- Movement: minutes
- Break before 3 pm: yes or no
- Phone rule followed: yes or no
- Boundary held today: yes or no

You will quickly see the pattern. On days you take better care of yourself, your voice is steadier. On days you skip them, you drift.

Jason's Turn

Two days after Jason tried thirty minutes of silence, he tried an hour. He sent a single message before the block began. I will be offline for an hour. If it is urgent and about safety, call 911. Otherwise, I will reply after 6. His hands shook as he typed. The sentence looked stark on the screen. He hit send. He put the phone in his bag and went for a slow walk to the deli and back. He felt every step like a small betrayal and a small victory.

When he returned, there were three messages. The first two were anxious. The last one was calmer. "I wrote the follow-up. Can you check it later?" He read them and felt an unfamiliar space open in his chest. He had not saved the day. He had not failed either. He had changed the sequence.

That night, he ate a real dinner. He turned off the lamp, closed his eyes, and listened to the apartment settle. The refrigerator hummed. A car door clicked. His phone lay face down again, and the quiet did not feel like a threat. It felt like a room with air.

Common Objections Answered

If I rest first, I will lose the moment to help.
You will shift the moment. You will move from frantic to steady. Most problems do not require a thirty-second response. They require a clear one.

If I say I am not available, she will feel abandoned.
She may feel afraid. You can validate the fear without changing the plan. "I hear that you feel alone. I am here after 6. Here is one step you can take now."

My job does not allow me to ignore my phone.
Build a rule that fits your reality. Silence one notification group, not all. Use a focus mode that only lets through work calls. Put non-urgent threads on a delay. There are ways to create more space for yourself—even if your work or family life requires a certain level of accessibility.

I tried boundaries before and it made things worse.
At first, boundaries can raise anxiety because they remove the quick fix. It is common and doesn't mean the boundaries will not be good for you and your person. Do not confuse discomfort with danger or failure.

Practice Plan for Week One

- **Day 1:** Pick your daily minimums and write them on a card where you can see them.
- **Day 2:** Create one phone rule that you can keep, even if it is only 15 minutes in the evening.
- **Day 3:** Try the 2-minute reset before responding to the first distress text.

- **Day 4:** Schedule one 10-minute walk without your phone before 3 pm.
- **Day 5:** Write your anchor sentence on paper and say it before you reply.
- **Day 6:** Choose one script and use it once.
- **Day 7:** Do the 5-minute audit. What worked? What needs adjusting?

At the end of the week, celebrate that you practiced. Not that you were perfect. The cycle you are changing was built with repetition over years. It may take time for lasting change to set in.

How Chapter 5 Connects to What Comes Next

When your oxygen is steady, you can hold warm limits without sounding cold. You can tolerate another person's distress without inhaling it. You can choose coaching over carrying. You can decide what you are available for and say it without guilt.

In Chapter 6, you will put this stability to work. We will talk more about how to **set boundaries without cruelty**, how to phrase them, when to deliver them, and how to hold them when pushback arrives.

For now, remember Jason in the mirror, practicing a simple sentence until it felt right. "I am not available for the next hour." Your own sentence will be different. It will feel strange at first. Then it will feel possible. Then it will feel like breathing.

CHAPTER 6

Setting Boundaries Without Cruelty

Most people do not struggle with boundaries because they do not understand them. They struggle because, to them, setting boundaries feels cruel.

This distinction matters because it reframes the problem entirely. If the issue was ignorance, education alone would solve it. A checklist would suffice. A few well-worded scripts would fix everything.

But if you are reading this book, you likely already know what a boundary *is*. You may have read articles about them. You may have tried to set them before. You may even be able to articulate, in theory, what a healthier dynamic would look like.

And yet, something keeps stopping you from building that healthier dynamic.

Chances are you already knew that something about your relationship felt unsustainable before you even picked up this book. You may not use that word. You may tell yourself it is just a difficult season, or that this is what commitment looks like, or that you simply need to be more patient. You may tell yourself that other people have it worse, or that love always involves sacrifice. But somewhere inside, there is a quiet recognition: the way things are structured right now is not right or healthy.

When people sit across from me in my office, and we begin talking about boundaries, there is often a visible shift before we even discuss specifics. Some people lean forward, relieved that the topic has finally been named. Others tense immediately. Their shoulders rise. Their voice changes. They look worried, even guilty, before we have said anything concrete at all.

Almost everyone says some version of the same sentence.

"I know I need boundaries. I just don't want to hurt them."

That sentence tells me a great deal.

It tells me that you are not indifferent to the person you love. You are not trying to control them. Nor are you looking for an excuse to disengage or withdraw. You are someone who cares deeply and has likely spent a long time organizing your life around keeping someone else steady.

It also tells me that you have learned, consciously or not, that love means availability. That being a good partner, child, or family member means absorbing discomfort so that someone else does not have to feel it.

This chapter is not about teaching you how to become harder, colder, or less available.

It is about helping you understand why boundaries feel so threatening in relationships shaped by dependency, and how to set limits that are firm without being cruel, loving without being self-erasing, and steady without abandoning either of you.

Why boundaries feel cruel in dependent relationships

In healthy relationships, boundaries are uncomfortable but understandable. One person may be disappointed. There may be frustration or negotiation. But both people can tolerate some level of discomfort without experiencing it as danger.

The disappointment does not feel existential. The relationship does not feel at risk simply because one person says no.

In dependent relationships, boundaries land very differently.

That is because the boundary is not just limiting a behavior. It is disrupting a system.

When someone depends on you for reassurance, emotional regulation, or decision-making, your availability becomes woven into how they function. Your presence lowers their anxiety. Your responses bring relief. Over time, that relief becomes something their nervous system expects.

Without anyone consciously choosing it, roles solidify. You become the stabilizing force. The person they reach for when something feels uncertain, uncomfortable, or overwhelming. The one who knows what to say, what to do, how to fix it, or how to make the feeling stop.

This often begins with kindness. You help because you can. You respond because it calms them. You step in because it feels easier than watching them struggle.

Over time, however, something subtle happens. Their tolerance for discomfort shrinks, while your responsibility for their comfort grows. When you introduce a boundary into that system, it does not register as a reasonable adjustment. It registers as loss.

This is why boundaries so often provoke panic, anger, or accusations of abandonment. Not because you are doing something wrong, but because the structure of the relationship is changing.

For the dependent person, the boundary feels like a withdrawal of safety. For you, it feels like an act of cruelty.

This is the bind.

I want to say this clearly because many people get stuck right here and turn back.

The intensity of someone's reaction to your boundary is not a reliable measure of whether the boundary is fair. Very often, it is a measure of how necessary the boundary is.

When a system has relied on you to function, it will protest when you try to make changes.

That protest does not mean you are doing something wrong. The system is simply adapting, and change is not always comfortable.

What a boundary actually is

Many people absorbed a distorted idea of boundaries long before they ever try to set one.

They imagine boundaries as walls. As ultimatums. As emotional withdrawal disguised as self-care. Something sharp and defensive that pushes other people away.

If that is what you think a boundary is, then of course it may feel cruel.

That understanding makes it almost impossible to set boundaries without feeling like a bad person because it frames boundaries as inherently rejecting. In your mind, you are left with two painful options: either remain endlessly accommodating or become someone you do not recognize, someone mean.

A boundary is not a wall. A boundary actually helps you stay loving and present with someone while also taking care of yourself. It is the structure that allows connection to exist without consuming the people inside it.

Walls keep people out, but containers can hold relationships together.

In dependent dynamics, boundaries are often the difference between a relationship that slowly collapses under its own weight and one that has a chance to breathe.

Without boundaries, relationships do not become more loving. They become more fragile. More rigid. More demanding. And eventually, more resentful.

This is where many well-intentioned people make a critical mistake. They assume that if the relationship feels strained, the solution must be more accommodation, more reassurance, more flexibility.

They think, *If I just explain better… If I just show up more… If I just sacrifice a little longer…*

But in relationships organized around dependency, more accommodation only creates more dependency.

Each time you remove discomfort for someone else, you reinforce the idea that discomfort is intolerable. Each time you step in to regulate emotions, solve problems, or make decisions, you rob someone of the ability to learn those skills for themselves. Perhaps paradoxically, over time boundaries can allow for more closeness. By creating space for your partner to learn to care for themselves, boundaries make it safer, healthier, and easier for you to be in close relationship with them. Thus, boundaries as a container—not a wall.

Why "being nice" fails as a strategy

Many people try to set boundaries by being exceptionally nice.

They soften their language. They overexplain. They apologize in advance. They frame their needs as temporary, conditional, or negotiable.

They hope that if they are gentle enough, the boundary will not hurt.

This often leads to confusion.

The dependent person hears uncertainty. They sense hesitation. They interpret softness as an opening. The boundary dissolves before it ever has a chance to take shape.

Clarity is kind. A boundary does not need to be harsh. But it does need to be real, definable, and firm.

The role boundaries play in preserving love

One of the most common fears people express is that boundaries will damage the relationship.

In reality, unspoken resentment damages relationships far more reliably than limits ever will.

When you say yes while feeling no, something inside you contracts. Over time, that contraction hardens. You may still show up physically, but emotionally, you begin to withdraw.

Boundaries, when held consistently, do the opposite. They prevent resentment from accumulating. They keep the relationship honest. They make room for genuine care instead of obligation.

A relationship without boundaries does not become closer. It becomes more rigid and brittle—and more likely to break.

The litmus test most people avoid

People often ask how to know when a boundary is truly needed. They expect a complicated answer, something nuanced or clinical.

It is not complicated.

Here is the simplest and most reliable litmus test I know:

Am I changing my plans, or am I changing my life?

Changing plans is part of any relationship. You reschedule dinner. You adjust your schedule during a hard week. You show up when someone needs extra support.

Changing your life is different.

Changing your life looks like:

- Cancelling commitments regularly to manage someone else's emotions
- Avoiding opportunities because they might provoke anxiety, jealousy, or distress
- Editing your words constantly to prevent a reaction
- Feeling like your time, energy, or attention is never truly yours
- Living in quiet anticipation of the next emotional emergency

The key difference is agency.

Changing plans is a choice.

Changing your life happens gradually, often without your awareness or consent.

When preserving the relationship requires you to reorganize who you are rather than simply adjust what you do, better boundaries are absolutely needed.

The invisible cost of changing your life

Many people do not recognize that they are changing their lives until the cost becomes impossible to ignore.

They notice it when they feel exhausted all the time. When they dread their phone buzzing. When they feel irritated at small requests but guilty for feeling that way. When they no longer recognize themselves in the mirror.

They may say, *I shouldn't feel this way. They're not doing anything wrong.*

Your partner likely does not intend to create these dynamics or constrain your life, but their intent is not relevant...

When your inner world becomes organized around preventing someone else's distress, your own needs slowly disappear from the equation.

Boundaries restore balance.

They reintroduce you as a person whose needs matter, too.

Boundaries are about responsibility, not control

Another common misunderstanding is that boundaries are about controlling the other person's behavior.

They are not.

Boundaries are about clarifying responsibility.

A boundary says:

- *This is what I am responsible for.*
- *This is what I am not responsible for.*

You are responsible for:

- Speaking clearly
- Acting consistently
- Regulating your own emotions

You are not responsible for:

- Preventing someone else's discomfort
- Managing their reactions
- Making sure they approve of your limits

When these roles are confused, dependency flourishes.

When they are clarified, growth becomes possible.

Why boundaries feel selfish at first

For people who are accustomed to prioritizing others, boundaries often feel selfish at first.

If you have spent years measuring your goodness by how much you can absorb, stepping back will feel wrong. Your nervous system has learned that your value lies in availability.

Boundaries challenge that belief.

They introduce a new idea: care does not require self-erasure.

It takes time for that idea to settle.

A quiet reframe

Instead of asking, *Is this boundary fair to them?*

Try asking, *Is this structure sustainable for me?*

Fairness without sustainability eventually becomes resentment.

Boundaries are not about winning or losing. They are about creating a structure in which both people can exist happily and thrive.

When boundaries move from helpful to essential

Not all boundary violations announce themselves loudly.

In fact, the most damaging ones rarely do.

They show up quietly, in small, repeated crossings that are easy to justify in the moment and hard to see clearly until you are already depleted.

You tell yourself:

- "It's easier if I just handle it."
- "They're too overwhelmed right now."
- "This isn't the time to push back."
- "If I don't respond, this will escalate."

Each of these thoughts makes sense in isolation. None of them are unreasonable. The problem is not the thought itself. The problem is what happens when these thoughts become the organizing logic of the relationship.

Over time, small accommodations accumulate. What began as kindness slowly becomes obligation. What began as support quietly turns into responsibility. And what began as love becomes something closer to management.

This is usually the point where people start to feel confused. They cannot point to a single dramatic incident. There was no explosion, no obvious betrayal, no clear moment where things went wrong. Yet, they feel trapped.

The benign versus malignant distinction

I sometimes use a medical analogy here because it helps people understand what is happening without blame.

A benign growth may be inconvenient. It may require monitoring. It may even need intervention. But it respects the surrounding tissue.

A malignant one does not.

It grows by crossing boundaries. It consumes what it touches. It does not recognize limits, because its survival depends on expansion.

Dependency becomes malignant when it no longer respects the individuality of the people involved.

This does not mean the dependent person is bad, selfish, or intentionally harmful. It means the *dynamic* has become harmful.

Malignant dependency shows up when:

- Your needs are consistently framed as unreasonable
- Your boundaries are treated as threats
- Your autonomy is experienced as abandonment
- Your exhaustion is ignored or minimized
- Your identity begins to shrink around the relationship

At this point, boundaries are no longer a tool for improvement. They are a requirement for survival.

The moment people miss

There is a particular moment many people overlook, and it is often the clearest signal that boundaries have moved from helpful to essential.

It is the moment when preserving the relationship requires you to betray yourself.

That betrayal can be subtle. It may look like:

- Silencing your frustration because it "isn't worth the fallout"
- Giving up opportunities to avoid someone else's anxiety
- Apologizing for needs you used to meet without guilt
- Feeling anxious when you imagine taking up space

You may tell yourself this is maturity. Or compromise. Or love.

But love that requires self-erasure is not sustainable.

And sustainability matters.

Red lines that are not negotiable

There are moments in relationships where flexibility is appropriate. There are also moments where clarity matters more than compassion.

The following are not gray areas. They are red lines.

- Repeated boundary violations after limits have been clearly stated
- Guilt, shame, or punishment for having needs
- Being made responsible for someone else's emotions or crises
- Escalation or retaliation when you say no
- Verbal abuse, threats, or intimidation
- Any form of physical harm or coercion
- Loss of autonomy, identity, or constant fear of conflict

If you recognize your relationship in this list, it is important to pause and seriously consider how your relationship's lack of boundaries is causing harm.

At that point, the question is no longer, *How do I set this boundary more gently?*

The question becomes, *how do I protect myself without?*

Why people stay past red lines

Many people stay far longer than they should, not because they are unaware of the damage, but because they feel morally trapped.

They think:

- "If I leave, I'm abandoning them."
- "If I enforce this boundary, they'll fall apart."

- "If I pull back, I'm proving I never really loved them."

These beliefs are powerful. They are also deeply misleading.

Staying in a dynamic that requires you to erase yourself does not make you loving. It makes you unavailable to your own life.

And paradoxically, it often prevents the other person from developing the strength they need.

The cost of waiting for clarity

Another reason people delay boundaries is the hope that things will get better on their own.

They wait for the "right moment." They wait for the crisis to pass. They wait for the other person to become more stable, more insight-oriented, more receptive.

What they often do not realize is that clarity rarely arrives *before* boundaries. It arrives *because* of them.

Boundaries create information.

They show you:

- How the other person handles frustration
- Whether they can tolerate limits
- Whether they respect your autonomy
- Whether the relationship can evolve

Without boundaries, you stay in ambiguity. With boundaries, the relationship reveals its true shape.

When compassion turns into enabling

One of the hardest shifts people have to make is recognizing when compassion has crossed into enabling.

Compassion says, *I care about your pain.*

Enabling says, *I will organize my life around preventing your pain.*

Boundaries return responsibility to where it belongs.

They say:

- *Your feelings matter.*
- *And so do mine.*
- *We each have work to do.*

A grounding truth

If you take nothing else from this section, take this:

A boundary becomes essential the moment your well-being becomes collateral damage.

That moment may not come with fireworks. It may arrive quietly, in exhaustion, resentment, or numbness.

You need to listen to those signals when they arrive. Your body and mind are trying to tell you that this relationship is not sustainable.

A clinical story from my training

During my fellowship, I worked with a patient whose story stayed with me because it captures how easily care turns into collapse.

He came in initially after a routine dental procedure. He had been prescribed pain medication, and on paper, everything looked straightforward. The prescription was appropriate. The procedure was minor. There were no red flags that suggested misuse at first glance. But as we talked, it became clear that the medication was not the real issue.

He was in his late twenties, professionally competent, thoughtful, and outwardly functional. What stood out almost immediately was his exhaustion. A kind of flattened vigilance. He spoke carefully as if every word might need to be justified.

When I asked about his life outside of work, he hesitated. Then he described his relationship.

His girlfriend was intensely dependent. She needed constant reassurance, constant contact, and constant proof that she was the priority. If he was unavailable, she panicked. If he set limits, she accused him of not loving her enough. If he tried to explain, she became overwhelmed and tearful.

At first, he responded the way many people do. He reassured. He adjusted. He stayed available. He told himself that this was what support looked like.

Over time, his world began to shrink.

He stopped seeing friends because it upset her. He avoided staying late at work because it triggered suspicion. He checked his phone compulsively, anticipating distress before it arrived. He lived in a near-constant state of alertness, bracing for the next emotional emergency.

When I asked him why he was taking more medication than prescribed, he did not say he was in pain.

He said, "It's the only way I feel calm enough to get through the day."

He was not chasing a high. He was trying to regulate a system that had become unbearable.

The medication misuse was a symptom of a deeper issue.

When we talked about boundaries, he became visibly anxious. He understood the concept intellectually. He could articulate what needed to change. But when we discussed actually pulling back, his fear surfaced immediately.

"But if I stop responding," he said, "she'll fall apart."

That fear keeps many people trapped far longer than they should be.

The illusion of responsibility

What made this case so instructive was not just the dependency itself, but the patient's sense of responsibility for it.

He believed, deeply, that his presence was the only thing keeping his girlfriend functional. He felt morally obligated to absorb her distress because the alternative felt dangerous.

This belief is common, but it is rarely accurate.

In many dependent relationships, the non-dependent partner confuses *influence* with *responsibility*. Yes, your actions affect the other person. That does not mean you are responsible for preventing every negative emotion they experience.

This confusion creates an impossible standard. You are expected to be endlessly available, endlessly soothing, endlessly patient, without ever needing anything in return.

Over time, those expectations become suffocating.

A contrasting case: boundaries that create growth

Not all stories end in collapse.

I also worked with a woman whose situation looked similar on the surface but unfolded differently.

She was in her forties, highly capable, and the primary support for an adult child who had never fully learned to function independently. Her child called multiple times a day, needed help with basic decisions, and became distressed whenever she tried to step back.

For years, she responded reflexively. She answered every call. She intervened in every problem. She told herself she was being a good parent.

Eventually, she reached a breaking point. Not because she stopped loving her child, but because she realized she was disappearing inside the role of mother.

With support, she began setting small, firm boundaries. She did not do it perfectly. She felt enormous guilt. Her child became angry and accused her of being uncaring.

But something else happened, too.

Without immediate rescue, the child began struggling in new ways. Then, slowly, began solving problems independently. Not gracefully. Not without setbacks. But genuinely.

The relationship changed.

It became less frantic. Less enmeshed. More honest.

This case illustrates something crucial: boundaries do not guarantee growth, but they do make it possible.

Why boundaries feel riskier than they are

In both cases, the fear was the same.

If I stop doing this, something terrible will happen.

That fear feels rational when you have been functioning as the emotional scaffolding in the relationship. You have evidence. When you step in, things calm down. When you pull back, things escalate.

But short-term escalation does not predict long-term collapse.

The nervous system resists change before it adapts to it.

This is why so many people misinterpret the initial backlash as proof that the boundary was wrong. They confuse discomfort with danger.

The role of guilt in keeping systems stuck

In the first case, guilt played a central role. The patient felt guilty for wanting space. Guilty for feeling resentful. Guilty for imagining a life that did not revolve around his girlfriend's needs.

That guilt was not a sign that he was a bad person for wanting more space. It was a sign that he was existing in an unhealthy, dependent system.

Guilt is often the emotional glue that holds dependent dynamics together.

It keeps the non-dependent person compliant. It frames autonomy as cruelty. It rewards self-erasure with temporary relief from guilty feelings.

Over time, boundaries weaken guilt's grip, but guilt does not go quietly.

What these cases teach us

These two cases are variations on the same theme.

In the first, boundaries were delayed until the costs became unbearable. In the second, boundaries were introduced before collapse.

Both cases show the same truth:

> Dependency does not resolve itself through more availability. It resolves, when it resolves at all, through better relationship structures.

> Boundaries are invitations to growth, responsibility, and differentiation. Whether the other person accepts that invitation is not something you can control, but without boundaries, the invitation is never even offered.

A final grounding thought

If you see yourself in these stories, you are not alone.

Many capable, compassionate people find themselves in similar positions, slowly carrying more than they realized they agreed to carry.

Boundaries can help you restore balance in your relationship.

They allow care to exist without collapse.

The predictable backlash cycle

When boundaries are introduced into dependent relationships, the response from the dependent person is rarely smooth, linear, or emotionally tidy.

Most people expect one of two outcomes. Either the other person will understand and adjust, or they will reject the boundary outright, and the relationship will end.

What actually happens is often far messier.

More often, boundaries trigger a **predictable backlash cycle**, one that unfolds in phases and catches people off guard if they are not prepared for it.

The cycle often looks like this:

- **First, panic.**
  The person feels destabilized. Their usual source of regulation has shifted. They may express fear, distress, or urgency that feels disproportionate to the situation.
- **Then, escalation.**
  Calls increase. Texts multiply. The tone becomes more intense. What once felt manageable now feels overwhelming.
- **Then, guilt and accusation.**
  You are told you are being cold, selfish, or uncaring. You may hear, "You've changed," or "I can't believe you'd do this to me."
- **Then, temporary improvement.**
  Apologies appear. Insight emerges. Promises are made. You may feel hopeful and relieved.
- **Then, regression.**
  Slowly, often quietly, the old patterns return.

This sequence is exhausting. It is emotionally destabilizing. And it is the reason many people abandon boundaries too early. They interpret escalation as evidence that the boundary was wrong or will never work.

Why backlash happens

Backlash does not mean you are hurting someone. It means a system that relied on your over-functioning is adjusting.

When you have been the primary regulator in a relationship, pulling back creates uncertainty. The other person must now tolerate emotions they previously outsourced to you.

Their tolerance does not develop instantly, but it will develop over time and only as they experience discomfort.

Backlash is the nervous system protesting change.

This is why demands for reassurance often intensify during early boundary-setting. The system is searching for the old equilibrium and testing whether the boundary is real or temporary.

If you retreat too quickly, the system learns an important lesson: escalation works.

The moment most people give up

There is a particular moment when many people abandon boundaries. It usually happens after the guilt phase.

They think:

- "Maybe I was too harsh."
- "Maybe I moved too fast."
- "They seem genuinely distressed."

This is the moment where compassion and fear blur together.

Giving up on your boundary may feel like kindness in that moment, but it is often avoidance. Avoidance of discomfort, conflict, or the risk of being seen as cruel.

Backing down is not kind. It only serves to reinforce dependence.

Why guilt gets louder before it fades

One of the most important things to understand about boundaries is that guilt often intensifies before it softens.

If you have spent years equating goodness with availability, withdrawing that availability will feel wrong at first. Your nervous system has been trained to associate someone else's relief with your value.

The guilt you feel is not evidence that you are doing harm. It is evidence that you are doing something unfamiliar.

This is why guilt is such a poor guide in dependent dynamics. It reflects conditioning, not real ethical decision-making.

What guilt is actually asking for

When guilt arises after a boundary is set, it is usually asking one of two things:

- *Make this discomfort stop.*
- *Restore the old role.*

Neither request serves growth.

Instead of responding to guilt by retreating on your boundary, respond by grounding yourself in the purpose of the boundary.

Ask:

- *What am I protecting by holding this line?*
- *What happens if I do nothing?*
- *Who disappears if I keep absorbing this?*

These questions anchor you in reality rather than emotion.

Normalizing the emotional chaos

It is important to normalize how disorienting this phase can feel.

People often report:

- Second-guessing themselves constantly
- Feeling emotionally raw or irritable
- Oscillating between confidence and doubt
- Wondering if they are becoming someone they do not like

None of this means you are doing it wrong.

The relationship is simply reorganizing, and a change in dependent systems is noisy and hard.

The difference between being firm and being cruel

One of the hardest distinctions for people to hold during backlash is the difference between firmness and cruelty.

Firmness is consistency without hostility.

Cruelty is using someone's distress as leverage.

You can be firm while still being kind. You can acknowledge fear without surrendering structure. You can hold a boundary without shaming or retaliating.

Firmness sounds like:

- "I hear how hard this is. I'm still keeping this limit."
- "I know you're upset. This boundary isn't changing."

Cruelty sounds like:

- "You're too much."
- "This is your problem."
- "If you can't handle this, that's on you."

You can hold a boundary firmly without ever speaking a cruel word.

Staying steady through the storm

Backlash feels like a storm because it disrupts predictability.

Your task during this phase is not to fix the storm, but to stay steady within it.

Steadiness comes from repetition. From saying the same thing calmly. From not introducing new explanations or exceptions under pressure.

The storm passes when the system learns that the boundary is real and survivable.

This does not mean the relationship will automatically improve, but over time, clarity may emerge.

A critical reassurance

I want to be very explicit here:

> **Backlash is not a sign you are doing damage. It is a sign that change is underway.**
>
> If you expect discomfort and prepare for it, you are far more likely to hold the boundary without becoming rigid or resentful.
>
> This is the crossing point. The chasm. The phase that determines whether the relationship evolves or remains stuck.
>
> Staying steady here is difficult but courageous.
>
> **Why guilt is such a poor guide**
>
> In many areas of life, guilt can be useful. It can alert us when we have crossed our own values or caused harm. But in dependent relationships, guilt often loses that function. It becomes distorted, amplified, and disconnected from reality.
>
> In these dynamics, guilt frequently operates as a withdrawal symptom.

You have trained yourself, over time, to equate your goodness with poor boundaries or with someone else's feelings of well-being. When someone else feels calm, reassured, or settled, you feel like a good person. When they feel distressed, anxious, or upset, you feel like you have failed.

Boundaries disrupt that equation.

They create a new experience that your nervous system is not used to tolerating:

- Someone else feels uncomfortable
- You allow that discomfort to exist

- You do not rush in to fix it

When this happens, guilt often spikes sharply. It can feel overwhelming, urgent, and morally charged. Many people interpret this as proof that they are being unkind. While understandable, it's untrue.

How guilt keeps dependency alive

In dependent systems, guilt plays a specific role. It keeps roles intact.

The dependent person learns, often unconsciously, that distress activates your care. You learn, just as unconsciously, that care means absorbing distress. Over time, guilt becomes the emotional mechanism that maintains this exchange.

When you set a boundary, guilt shows up to pull you back into the familiar role.

It says:

- "You're hurting them."
- "You're abandoning them."
- "This isn't who you are."

But notice what guilt does *not* ask:

- "Is this sustainable?"
- "Is this fair to you?"
- "What happens you don't act in this moment?"

Guilt is reactive. It is oriented toward immediate relief, not long-term health.

That is why it is such a poor guide.

The danger of mistaking guilt for empathy

Many people confuse guilt with empathy.

Empathy allows you to understand and care about someone else's pain without taking responsibility for it. Guilt collapses that distinction. It tells you that if someone is hurting, you must be at fault.

This confusion leads people to override their own limits in the name of compassion.

But compassion without boundaries quickly turns into self-erasure.

True empathy says, *I see your pain.*

Guilt says, *Your pain is my responsibility.*

Only one of those allows both people to remain intact.

What happens when you ignore guilt

Another fear people carry is that if they stop listening to guilt, they will become selfish or uncaring.

This fear is understandable, especially if you have spent years orienting toward others.

In practice, what usually happens is the opposite.

When people stop letting guilt dictate their behavior, they often become more genuinely present. Less resentful. Less reactive. More capable of offering real care instead of obligatory care.

Guilt-driven care is brittle. It breaks under pressure. Boundary-based care is steadier.

Holding limits without becoming cruel

This is the part many books gloss over.

They tell you to "set boundaries" but not how to *hold* them when emotions surge, accusations fly, or guilt screams for relief.

Holding a boundary requires clarity.

Clarity sounds like:

- "I care about you, and I'm not available right now."
- "I can talk later, not in this moment."

- "I'm here to support you, not to take this over."

Notice what these statements share. They acknowledge care *and* state a limit. They do not apologize for existing. They do not invite debate.

What clarity does **not** sound like:

- Over-explaining your reasons
- Justifying your needs
- Arguing your case
- Apologizing for having limits

Over-explaining is often an attempt to manage the other person's emotions. It comes from the hope that if you say it just right, they won't feel hurt.

But boundaries that depend on the other person's approval are not boundaries. They are requests.

Why over-explaining backfires

When guilt is high, people often try to make boundaries painless. They soften language. They provide context. They anticipate objections and respond to them in advance.

Ironically, this often makes things worse.

Over-explaining teaches two unintended lessons:

1. That your boundary is negotiable
2. That the other person's distress determines whether it holds

In an attempt to reduce anxiety, over-explaining often increases it. The dependent person hears uncertainty and pushes for more reassurance.

Clarity, not elaboration, creates stability.

You are allowed to state a boundary without convincing anyone it is reasonable.

What steadiness actually looks like

Steadiness is often misunderstood as emotional flatness.

In reality, steadiness means:

- Saying the same thing calmly
- Not escalating when the other person does
- Not introducing new explanations under pressure
- Allowing feelings without fixing them

Steadiness is boring. Repetitive. Unimpressive.

And that is exactly why it works.

Dependent systems thrive on intensity. Steadiness starves the cycle.

A quiet permission

If you have been relying on guilt to guide your decisions, it may feel unsettling to step away from it.

So here is the permission many people need but rarely receive:

> You are allowed to let guilt be present without obeying it.
>
> You are allowed to feel uncomfortable without changing course.
>
> You are allowed to care deeply without sacrificing yourself.

Boundaries do not make you cruel. They make you real.

Scripts that protect you while staying loving

Scripts are not about controlling the conversation.

They are about protecting *you* from over-functioning when pressure rises.

When emotions escalate, most people do not suddenly become eloquent. They become reactive. They explain too much, soften too quickly, or abandon the boundary entirely in an effort to restore calm.

Scripts remove the need to improvise.

Your goal is not to say the perfect thing. It is to say something **simple, repeatable, and steady enough** that you do not have to renegotiate your limits every time someone feels distressed.

Think of scripts as guardrails. They keep you from sliding back into old roles when guilt, fear, or urgency takes over.

Below are common scenarios, paired with language that protects the relationship *and* your autonomy.

When reassurance texts keep coming

This is one of the most common and seductive entry points into dependency.

The text itself is often vague.

> "I don't feel okay."
>
> "Can you talk?"
>
> "Are you mad at me?"

The unspoken message is clear: *I can't settle without you.*

If you respond immediately and repeatedly, you become the external regulator. Relief arrives only through you.

A boundary here sounds like:

- "I see that you're overwhelmed. I'm offline right now. We can talk later."
- "I'm not available to text back and forth. I'll check in this evening."

What to avoid:

- Answering "just this once"
- Explaining why you are unavailable
- Engaging in prolonged reassurance

Predictability matters more than explanation. When your responses are consistent, the nervous system begins to adapt to a new normal.

When they want you to decide for them

Dependency often shows up as decision paralysis.

"What should I do?"

"I don't know what to choose."

"Just tell me what you think."

At first, it feels helpful to answer. You know them well. You want to ease their anxiety. But over time, decision-making migrates outward. You become their executive function.

A boundary here is subtle but essential.

Instead of answering the question, redirect responsibility:

- "I can help you think this through, but I'm not going to decide for you."
- "What options are you considering?"

If they say they don't know:

- "Pick one small step. You don't need to get it right."

Coaching restores agency. Making decisions for them erodes it.

Expect frustration at first. You are removing a shortcut their nervous system has relied on.

When emotional dumping happens late at night

Late-night emotional crises feel intimate and urgent. They also quietly destroy your capacity.

Sleep deprivation lowers patience, increases resentment, and makes boundaries harder to hold the next day.

A boundary here protects your nervous system.

- "I care about this, and I'm not available late at night."

- "Let's talk tomorrow."

Notice what you are *not* doing. You are not dismissing the issue. You are not minimizing their feelings. You are simply choosing better timing for you.

Exhaustion is not a prerequisite for love.

When work keeps getting interrupted

Work interference often becomes normalized in dependent dynamics.

Texts during meetings. Calls during deadlines. Emotional crises that demand immediate attention, regardless of context.

Boundaries here are logistical, not emotional.

- "I don't respond to personal messages during work hours."
- "If something is truly urgent, call. Otherwise, I'll respond after work."

Logistical boundaries are often easier to hold because they are less personal. They also teach an important lesson: your life does not pause on demand.

When you're accused of abandoning them

Accusations like:

- "You're abandoning me."
- "You don't care anymore."
- "You've changed."

are attempts to restore the old system.

Respond to the feeling without surrendering the boundary:

- "I hear that you're scared. I'm still keeping this boundary."
- "I'm not leaving. I'm changing how I show up."

Do not argue with the accusation. Do not defend your character. Do not prove your love.

Repeat the limit.

When they say, "You've changed"

They are often right.

Change is the point.

- "Yes, I have. I'm taking better care of myself."
- "This change is important to me."

Growth will always feel like loss to someone who benefited from things staying the same.

The temptation to soften too much

When people first start using scripts, they often try to soften them excessively.

They add disclaimers:

- "I feel terrible saying this…"
- "I know this is hard for you…"
- "I don't want you to think I don't care…"

While well-intentioned, this often undermines the boundary.

It shifts focus back to managing the other person's reaction instead of holding your boundary.

Using warmth without overfunctioning

Warmth can exist without rescue.

Warmth sounds like:

- A calm tone
- A steady voice
- Consistent language

Warmth does not require:

- Endless reassurance

- Emotional overexertion
- Immediate availability

You can be kind without being consumed.

What to expect when scripts start working

When scripts are used consistently, several things often happen:

- Initial escalation
- Accusations or guilt-inducing language
- Attempts to negotiate exceptions
- Eventual reduction in intensity

Things often escalate before they begin to get better. The system resists change. Consistently enforcing your boundaries through this period of escalation can be difficult, but it's critical. If you remain consistent, the scripts will start to work, and the intensity of your partner's reaction will begin to lessen.

When the boundary breaks

At some point, your boundary will break.

You will answer a text you meant to ignore.

You will stay on the call longer than you planned.

You will step in to solve something you had decided not to take over.

This doesn't mean you are a bad person or are incapable of holding boundaries. You're simply human, and change is difficult. Building new habits takes time.

One of the most damaging myths around boundaries is the idea that they must be held perfectly to matter. That belief turns boundary-setting into a brittle, high-stakes performance. When people inevitably fall short, they conclude that the entire effort has failed, and they give up prematurely.

You're going to slip up at some point. It's almost inevitable. Expect to make mistakes, especially early on, and make sure you have a plan for what to do next.

Why people panic after a boundary slip

When a boundary breaks, people often experience a surge of shame.

They think:

- "I ruined it."
- "Now they'll expect this again."
- "I proved I don't really mean it."

Shame pushes people toward extremes and polarized thinking. They either overcorrect by becoming rigid and harsh, or they give up entirely and return to old patterns.

Neither response is necessary.

Boundaries are not contracts. They are practices.

And practices improve through repetition, not perfection.

The repair sequence that actually works

Repair is where boundaries become durable.

Without repair, boundaries feel fragile. With repair, they become resilient.

Here is a repair sequence that works in real life.

1. **Name what happened internally**

   Before you say anything to the other person, pause and be honest with yourself.

   Ask:

   - "Why did I step in?"
   - "What was I trying to avoid?"

Often the answer is something like:

- "I was tired."
- "I felt guilty."
- "I was afraid of escalation."

Naming this internally prevents self-punishment. It keeps you grounded in reality instead of judgment.

2. Regulate yourself before responding

If you respond while flooded with shame or fear, you will either over-explain or retreat.

Take a breath. Give yourself a moment to settle.

You are not behind. Nothing catastrophic has happened.

3. Restate the boundary clearly

This is the step many people skip, and it is the most important one.

A repair sounds like:

- "Last night I stepped in when I said I wouldn't."
- "Going forward, I'm sticking to the plan."

Notice what is missing.

There is no apology for the boundary itself.

There is no justification.

There is no invitation to renegotiate.

You are correcting course, not confessing wrongdoing.

4. Resume without apology

Apologies imply harm. You did not cause harm by reasserting a boundary.

You are allowed to say:

- "I'm going back to the boundary we discussed."
- "This is still important to me."

Repair teaches the nervous system that boundaries can bend without breaking.

Why repair builds trust

Many people fear that acknowledging a boundary slip will undermine their credibility.

In practice, the opposite is true.

A properly managed boundary slip can actually build trust because it demonstrates:

- Self-awareness
- Consistency over time
- Commitment to structure, not impulse

Dependent systems often operate on all-or-nothing logic. Either you are fully available, or you are abandoning. Repair introduces a third option: *I am imperfect and still committed.*

That third option is where growth happens.

Discomfort is not danger

One of the reasons boundary slips feel so urgent is fear of misjudging a crisis.

People worry:

- "What if this was actually serious?"
- "What if I ignored something dangerous?"

That fear is understandable but is often misapplied.

Not all distress is a crisis.

In dependent dynamics, discomfort is frequently experienced as intolerable. Anxiety rises quickly. Language escalates. Everything feels urgent. But feelings are not facts.

Someone's internal experience of extreme distress does not automatically mean something dangerous is happening.

Learning to tell the difference between discomfort and danger is essential for holding boundaries without guilt.

How to tell discomfort from a true crisis

When deciding whether to intervene fully or hold the line, ask yourself these questions slowly and honestly.

First: Is there an immediate risk to life or safety?
Statements about self-harm, medical emergencies, threats of violence, or situations involving children or legal danger always override boundaries. In those moments, you intervene. You call for help. You act. Boundaries resume after safety is restored.

Second: Is this a new situation, or a familiar loop?
True crises tend to be unpredictable. Dependent crises are often repetitive. If the timing, language, and emotional arc feel identical to the last several "emergencies," you are likely dealing with distress rather than danger.

Third: Would this be solvable if I were unavailable?
If the answer is yes, even if it would be uncomfortable or messy, it is not a crisis. It is an opportunity for growth.

Fourth: Does stepping in teach dependence or stability?
If your involvement lowers anxiety in the moment but prevents learning, you are rescuing rather than helping.

Holding a boundary in moments of discomfort is not abandonment. It is refusing to confuse distress with catastrophe.

Ethical clarity

It bears repeating plainly, because people often need to hear it more than once.

You are not your loved one's therapist.

Love does not require constant availability.

Kindness without structure becomes harm.

By setting boundaries, you are protecting the conditions under which both of you can function and thrive.

A stabilizing perspective

If you find yourself slipping, repairing, questioning, and trying again, you are not failing.

You are learning.

Boundaries are not held once. They are held repeatedly, imperfectly, and with increasing steadiness over time.

Boundary-planning worksheet

Boundaries are hardest to invent in the moment they are needed.

When emotions rise, old reflexes take over. You explain too much. You soften too quickly. You abandon the limit without fully realizing you have done so.

This worksheet is designed to slow that process down.

It is not meant to be perfect. It is meant to give you something solid to return to when pressure builds.

Use it before the next predictable moment of strain, not in the middle of it.

Step 1: The situation that needs a boundary

Be specific. Vague boundaries fail.

Examples:

- Late-night emotional dumping
- Repeated reassurance texts during work
- Being asked to make decisions they avoid

Write it out clearly.

Step 2: The boundary

One clear sentence. No explanations. No qualifiers.

Examples:

- "I'm not available to talk late at night."
- "I won't make this decision for you."
- "I don't respond to personal messages during work hours."

If the boundary takes more than one sentence, it is probably a justification, not a boundary.

Step 3: The likely reaction

Anticipating the reaction helps you stay steady.

Common reactions include:

- Panic
- Guilt-inducing language
- Anger
- Escalation
- Temporary compliance followed by regression

Write down what you realistically expect, not what you hope for.

Step 4: Your response to that reaction

This is where many people freeze.

Prepare one or two repeatable responses that acknowledge emotion without surrendering structure.

Examples:

- “I hear how hard this is. I’m still keeping this boundary.”
- “I know you’re upset. This limit isn’t changing.”

You are not trying to convince. You are trying to remain consistent.

Step 5: Your self-support plan

Boundaries cost energy. Plan for that.

Ask yourself:

- How will I regulate after holding this line?
- Who can I check in with?
- What helps me settle when guilt spikes?

Self-support is not indulgence. It is maintenance.

Step 6: The red line

Name what would signal that the situation requires more support or distance.

Examples:

- Repeated retaliation after limits are stated
- Escalation into verbal abuse
- Threats or coercion
- Loss of personal safety

Red lines protect you from rationalizing harm.

A filled example

Situation:

My partner sends multiple reassurance texts during the workday and becomes distressed if I don’t respond immediately.

Boundary:
"I don't respond to personal messages during work hours."

Likely reaction:
Panic and accusations of not caring.

My response:
"I hear that you're upset. I'll talk with you after work."

Self-support plan:
Take a short walk during lunch. Text a friend who knows what I'm working on. Remind myself why this boundary matters.

Red line:
Escalation into insults or threats.

This is not rigid. It is grounding.

Why writing this down matters

Boundaries held only in your head are easier to abandon.

Writing boundaries down does something important. It shifts them from emotional reactions to intentional choices.

It also gives you something to return to when doubt creeps in.

Because doubt will creep in.

You will have moments where you wonder if you are being unfair, cold, or selfish. In those moments, return to what you wrote when you were calm.

A quiet closing

If boundaries have felt cruel to you, it is not because you lack compassion.

It is because you have been carrying too much for too long.

You were never meant to be the sole regulator of another adult's emotional world. You were never meant to disappear inside your care for someone else. You are allowed to build a life that belongs to you.

In the next chapter, we will focus on communication. Not as persuasion, and not as appeasement, but as clarity. Because boundaries hold best when your words are simple, steady, and honest.

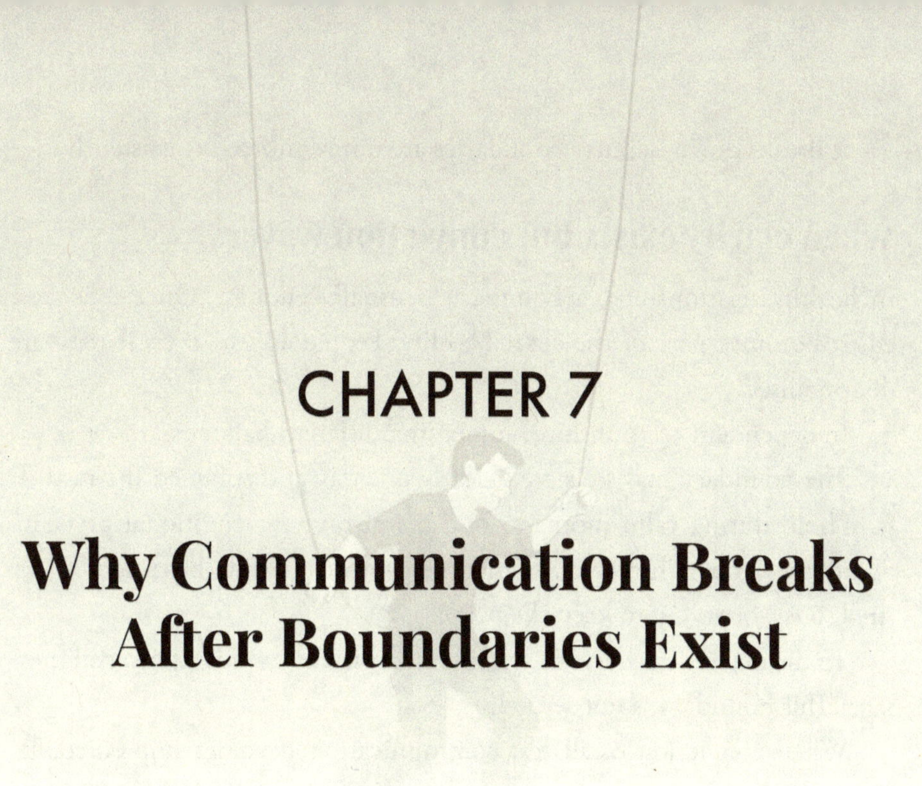

CHAPTER 7

Why Communication Breaks After Boundaries Exist

Section 1

By the time most people reach this chapter, they already understand something important.

They know a boundary is needed.

They may have even set one.

And yet, despite that clarity, the relationship still feels unstable.

Conversations spiral. Emotions escalate. The same issues resurface again and again, often with more intensity than before. You may leave these interactions feeling drained, confused, or strangely guilty, even though you were clear about your limit.

This is where many people assume they are doing something wrong.

They think they chose the wrong words. Or that they were not gentle enough. Or that they should have explained more carefully so the other person would finally understand.

But communication does not break down in dependent dynamics because people fail to talk well.

It breaks down because boundaries are not reinforced consistently.

When clarity exists but conviction wavers

In healthy relationships, a boundary is usually enough. Once it is stated, it becomes part of the shared reality. People adjust, even if they are disappointed.

In dependent relationships, something different happens.

The boundary may be stated clearly one day and softened the next. It may hold during calm moments and dissolve under emotional pressure. Sometimes you reinforce it. Sometimes you let it slide because you are tired, busy, or trying to keep the peace.

To the dependent nervous system, inconsistency sends a powerful message: This boundary is not settled.

When conviction oscillates, communication becomes unpredictable. The other person learns, often unconsciously, that persistence works. They test. They push. They return to the topic from new angles, hoping for a different outcome.

Over time, the relationship organizes itself around this uncertainty.

Why inconsistency fuels escalation

Many people believe that being flexible will make communication smoother.

In dependent dynamics, flexibility often has the opposite effect.

When boundaries are inconsistently reinforced, the dependent person does not feel safer. They feel more anxious. They do not know which version of you they will encounter. Calm, firm, accommodating, or apologetic.

That uncertainty increases anxiety.

The conversation grows louder. Emotions intensify. The pressure to explain, justify, or reassure increases. What began as a simple limit turns into an ongoing negotiation because they have learned that testing your boundaries works.

The trap of trying to be understood

At this stage, many people shift their goal without realizing it.

Instead of holding the boundary, they try to be understood.

They explain their reasoning in more detail. They revisit the same points with new language. They respond to objections as if the issue were a misunderstanding rather than a decision.

This instinct is understandable. Being misunderstood hurts.

But in boundary conversations, trying to be understood often undermines conviction.

Each explanation subtly reopens the discussion. Each clarification signals that the boundary might still be up for debate. Each attempt to persuade teaches the other person that agreement is required for the boundary to hold.

It isn't.

You do not need consensus to have a limit.

How communication becomes the new battleground

Once a boundary is set, communication becomes the primary testing ground.

The dependent person may not challenge the boundary directly. Instead, they challenge it indirectly:

- Through emotion
- Through urgency
- Through guilt
- Through repetition

Conversation becomes the arena where the old system tries to reassert itself.

This is why so many people say, "I set the boundary, but everything got worse."

What actually got worse was not the boundary.

It was the communication around it.

A necessary shift

Chapter 6 focused on understanding boundaries and why they are essential.

This chapter focuses on something different:

How to communicate once the boundary exists without being pulled back into dependent cycles.

The goal is not to say more.
It is to say less, more clearly.

The goal is not to persuade.
It is to reinforce.

The goal is not to resolve every conversation.
It is to end them cleanly.

The rest of this chapter will show you how to do that, step by step, without becoming cold, cruel, or disconnected.

Section 2: Clarity Beats Persuasion

When boundaries start to wobble, most people do not panic because they doubt the boundary.

They panic because the other person does not agree that the boundary is valid, important, or necessary.

The moment disagreement appears, many people shift their goal without realizing it. They stop holding the boundary and start trying to convince.

They explain their reasoning more carefully. They offer additional context. They anticipate objections and respond to them in advance. They hope that if the other person truly understands, the tension will dissolve.

This reflex is deeply human. We are wired to seek understanding, especially from people we care about.

But in dependent dynamics, persuasion undermines conviction.

The false promise of explanation

Explanation feels responsible. It feels fair. It feels kind.

"If I can just explain why this matters to me," people think, "they'll stop pushing."

In practice, the opposite often happens.

Each explanation extends the conversation. Each justification invites a counterargument. Each attempt to be understood subtly reframes the boundary as a proposal rather than a decision.

This is how communication becomes a negotiation, even when no one intends it to.

Why over-explaining increases pressure

Over-explaining does not reduce anxiety in dependent systems. It increases it.

When language keeps changing, the nervous system keeps scanning for openings. When reasons multiply, the boundary feels conditional. When tone shifts under pressure, the system learns that persistence works.

Dependent dynamics are exquisitely sensitive to inconsistency. The moment conviction wavers, pressure increases. Over-explaining can create inconsistency and thus increase pressure from the dependent person.

Dialogue versus decision

There is an important distinction that many people never learn to make.

Some conversations are dialogues.

Some conversations are decisions.

Dialogue invites input, collaboration, and compromise. Decisions communicate a settled position.

Problems arise when people present decisions as dialogues.

They ask questions they are not actually open to reconsideration. They explain boundaries as if they are still up for debate. They respond to objections as if agreement is required for the boundary to stand.

This creates confusion and resentment on both sides.

Clarity requires honesty about which mode you are in.

If something is a decision, it must be communicated as one.

Stating is not shutting down

Many people fear that stating a boundary plainly is rude, cold, or authoritarian.

In reality, stating a boundary clearly is respectful. It does not manipulate. It does not cajole. It does not pretend something is negotiable when it isn't.

Stating sounds like:

- "This is what I'm going to do."
- "This is my limit."
- "This decision isn't changing."

Stating does not require:

- Long explanations
- Emotional persuasion
- Agreement from the other person

You can state a boundary while still acknowledging emotion. You simply do not let emotion redefine the structure or the boundary.

The cost of trying to be understood

The desire to be understood is powerful. But when being understood becomes a requirement for holding a boundary, you hand control of your limits to someone else's approval. Boundaries are about what you will do in response to a certain behavior, not about someone else's actions, reactions, or feelings. Instead of asking, "How do I explain this better?" try asking: "Have I already been clear?" If the answer is yes, more explanation is unlikely to help. You do not need to convince someone in order to set a boundary.

You only need to be clear and then remain consistent. Everything else will build from that foundation.

A quiet anchor

Section 3: Saying Less Without Sounding Cold

Once people accept that persuasion undermines conviction, a new fear often appears.

"If I stop explaining," they worry, "I'll sound harsh."

"If I say less," they fear, "I'll seem uncaring."

"If I don't soften this," they think, "I'll hurt them."

This fear keeps many people talking long after clarity has already been achieved. People add qualifiers, context, and reassurance not because they are needed but because they reduce their own discomfort in the moment. Saying more feels gentler. It feels responsible. It feels like proof of care.

They talk because they are afraid of being seen as cruel.

Why being "nice" backfires

Many people try to set boundaries by being exceptionally nice.

They soften their language. They frame their needs as temporary. They hedge their statements with uncertainty.

"I just need a little space right now."

"I don't want you to think I don't care."

"Maybe we can figure out something that works for both of us."

These statements are not unkind. But they are unclear.

To the dependent nervous system, softness signals possibility. It suggests that the boundary might be flexible, negotiable, or provisional.

Being nice does not create safety when structure is missing. Clarity does.

Empathy without surrender

Empathy is not the enemy of boundaries, but when empathy is used to reopen decisions that should be settled, it creates confused boundaries and roles. You can say:

- "I know this is hard."
- "I understand why you're upset."
- "I can hear how much this matters to you."

And still say:

- "This boundary stands."
- "I'm not changing my decision."
- "We'll talk later."

Empathy paired with non-negotiability is stabilizing. It allows you to be warm without letting boundaries slip.

The internal discipline of fewer words

Saying less requires tolerating discomfort and not filling the space. It requires resisting the urge to explain, justify, or reassure in order to calm yourself.

This is especially difficult for people who have learned to regulate others as a way of regulating themselves. Silence can feel dangerous when you are used to talking your way out of tension.

But silence, when paired with clarity, is often the most powerful part of communication.

What not to say

There are certain phrases that undermine boundaries and damage trust.

Avoid:

- Character attacks: "You're too much," "You're being unreasonable"

- Dismissive language: "That's your problem"
- Frustration leaks: "I can't deal with this anymore"
- Moralizing: "Any reasonable person would understand this"

These statements escalate defensiveness and shift the conversation away from structure. Boundaries should never be enforced through humiliation or punishment.

A steady alternative

Saying less does not mean saying nothing.

It means choosing words that do not invite negotiation.

Examples:

- "I've been clear about my boundary."
- "I'm not continuing this conversation right now."
- "This isn't changing."

These statements may feel abrupt at first. That discomfort is not cruelty. It is unfamiliarity.

A grounding reminder

You are not responsible for how long a conversation lasts.

You are responsible for whether your words match your intention.

When clarity is present, fewer words are not colder.

They are kinder.

Section 4: Permission to Pause, Close, or Defer Conversations

One of the most destabilizing beliefs people carry into boundary conversations is the idea that a conversation must end in resolution to be ethical.

They believe that stopping too soon is unkind. That pausing is avoidance. That closing a conversation before the other person feels better is a form of abandonment.

This belief keeps many people trapped in conversations that have already stopped being productive.

In dependent dynamics, insisting on resolution often serves to undermine your conviction in holding your boundaries.

Why conversations loop instead of conclude

Conversations in dependent relationships rarely end naturally. Instead, they loop.

The same points are raised again and again, often with increasing intensity. Every pass through the loop raises the emotional stakes. What began as a discussion turns into an endurance test.

These conversation loops happen because the system is searching for stability and relief from tension. The dependent person seeks regulation. The non-dependent person seeks calm.

Talking becomes the tool both rely on to seek a safer emotional space even when it has stopped working.

At that point, more communication will not create understanding or stability. It's better to stop there and revisit the conversation later if needed. Hopefully, when you're both in a more regulated space.

Avoidance versus containment

Many people worry that ending a conversation with unresolved feelings is a form of avoidance, but that's an oversimplification. Ending an unproductive conversation is not avoidance, and you very well may return to the conversation later. Going in circles with each other is simply unproductive.

Containment has three elements:

1. Naming what is happening
2. Reaffirming the boundary

3. Setting a clear pause point

Avoidance leaves the other person guessing.

Containment leaves them oriented.

Examples of containment:

- "We're going in circles."
- "I've been clear about my boundary."
- "I'm pausing this conversation now."

Containment protects the relationship from erosion.

Permission without justification

Here is a permission many people need to hear explicitly:

You are allowed to pause a conversation even if the other person is upset.

You are allowed to close a conversation even if they disagree.

You are allowed to defer a conversation even if they insist it is urgent.

You do not owe resolution in the moment.

Resolution pursued under emotional pressure is rarely real. It is usually compliance.

Clean stopping language

Stopping cleanly means pairing empathy with non-negotiability.

It sounds like:

- "I hear how frustrated you are, and I'm still keeping this boundary."
- "I understand this feels urgent. I'm not continuing this conversation right now."
- "We can revisit this later. I'm stopping here."

Notice what these statements do not include:

- Apologies for the boundary

- Long explanations
- Invitations to negotiate

They acknowledge the dependent person's emotion without reorganizing your behavior around it.

Why stopping often feels cruel

For people who have been conditioned to stay, stopping feels wrong.

Your nervous system may interpret the other person's distress as danger. Guilt may surge. The urge to explain may become overwhelming.

These difficult feelings do not mean you are doing something wrong.

It means you are interrupting a familiar pattern.

Staying past the point of effectiveness does not make you kind. It harms you both.

Stopping cleanly teaches a different lesson:

- Emotions can rise without rescue
- Boundaries remain intact under pressure
- Connection does not require collapse

Section 5: Responding to Emotion Without Being Pulled In

For many people, the most difficult part of setting boundaries is not identifying your needs and limits or having that initial conversation. It is the emotional response that follows.

Crying, anger, and accusations. Collapse. Raised voices, or long silences that feel heavy and punishing.

In these moments, even people who know intellectually what they need and why often abandon the new structure they're trying to build. They soften, explain, or retreat. Not because they doubt their boundary, but because they feel responsible for the emotional intensity in the room.

This is where dependent dynamics regain control.

What escalation is really testing

Emotional escalation is rarely about the content of the conversation.

It is a test of consistency.

When the nervous system senses that its usual source of regulation has shifted, it reacts urgently. It raises the emotional volume in an attempt to restore the old pattern.

Consciously or not, they are testing whether the boundary will hold.

If your response changes based on emotional intensity, the system learns that escalation works.

Being an anchor, not an absorber

Many people try to absorb emotion in order to calm it.

They reassure. They soothe. They problem-solve. They stay longer than they should.

This response only creates further dependence. It undermines the goals of setting boundaries in the first place.

Being an anchor means staying steady while emotions move around you.

An anchor:

- Speaks calmly
- Uses fewer words
- Repeats rather than varies language
- Does not escalate in response to escalation

You do not argue with emotion but allow it to exist without reorganizing around it.

Responding to crying or emotional collapse

Crying can feel like an emergency. It activates care, guilt, and urgency all at once. Many people interpret tears as proof that they have caused harm. They haven't. Crying is a signal of distress, not wrongdoing.

A grounded response sounds like:

- "I can see how painful this feels."
- "I know this is overwhelming."
- "I'm still holding the boundary."

What to avoid:

- Rushing to reassure
- Offering solutions to stop the tears
- Changing the boundary to restore calm
- Apologizing for the limit itself

Your steadiness is more regulating than rescue.

Responding to anger or raised voices

Anger often triggers defensiveness. People feel compelled to explain, justify, or prove their intentions.

This impulse is understandable.

It is also counterproductive.

When anger escalates:

- Lower your voice
- Shorten your sentences
- Restate the boundary

Examples:

- "I'm not continuing this conversation if voices are raised."
- "I hear that you're angry. I'm still keeping this limit."

- "We can talk when this is calmer."

If anger continues to escalate, disengaging is not cruelty.

It is containment.

Naming escalation without shaming

You are allowed to name what is happening.

Naming is not accusing.

It is orienting.

Examples:

- "This is starting to feel heated."
- "We're going in circles."
- "This conversation isn't productive right now."

Naming escalation shifts the focus from content to process and gives both people a chance to reset.

Why staying longer often makes things worse

Many people believe that if they stay long enough, the other person will eventually calm down.

In dependent dynamics, staying often reinforces escalation.

The nervous system learns:

- Intensity keeps connection
- Distress keeps engagement
- Regulation comes from you

Leaving calmly and predictably teaches a different lesson:

- Emotions can be tolerated
- Boundaries remain intact
- Connection does not require collapse

A grounding reminder

You are not responsible for managing another adult's emotional surge.

You are responsible for how you show up inside it.

Staying anchored does more for long-term stability than any perfectly worded explanation ever could.

Section 6: Structure Creates Safety (The DESC Framework)

By this point in the chapter, you may notice something important.

None of what you have read so far requires better emotional intelligence, deeper empathy, or more insight. You already have those.

What it requires is **structure**.

Most boundary conversations collapse because people lack a framework to hold boundaries steady once pressure rises. When emotions escalate, language loosens. Conviction wavers. Explanations multiply. What was clear becomes negotiable.

Learning and committing to new structures in your relationships and communication prevents that slide.

It gives you something solid to return to when guilt, fear, or urgency start pulling you off course. When communication lacks structure, it becomes reactive. You start responding to emotion instead of holding decisions. You say more, not because more is needed, but because silence feels risky.

To the dependent nervous system, this variability sends a clear signal: The boundary is not settled.

Structure communicates the opposite:

This is clear. This has been thought through. This is not up for renegotiation.

One of the most effective and practical structures for boundary communication is the **DESC framework**.

What the DESC framework is (and what it is not)

The DESC framework is widely used in behavioral health, leadership training, and conflict resolution because it keeps communication grounded, concise, and non-reactive.

DESC is not a script to recite.

It is a **container** that helps you say less and mean more.

DESC stands for:

- **D — Describe**
- **E — Express**
- **S — Specify**
- **C — Consequence**

Each step has a distinct function. Skipping or weakening any part undermines conviction.

D — Describe (facts, not interpretations)

The first step is to describe what is happening without judgment, analysis, or motive.

This anchors the conversation in reality.

In observable terms, describe what happened and when it happened.

Examples:

- "You've been texting me multiple times during work hours."
- "Our conversations often go late into the night."
- "Decisions get redirected back to me…"

Avoid:

- "You're too dependent."

- "You don't respect my time."
- "You always need reassurance."

Descriptions reduce defensiveness and prevent the conversation from becoming about character or intent.

E — Express (impact, not accusation)

Next, express how the situation affects you.

Examples:

- "I feel distracted and overwhelmed."
- "I start to feel resentful."
- "I feel pressured and anxious."

Notice what is missing:

- "You make me feel…"
- "If you didn't do this…"

Expressing impact keeps empathy intact without surrendering responsibility.

S — Specify (the boundary clearly)

This is the most important step — and the one most often weakened.

You need to state the boundary plainly, without conditions, hedging, or negotiation.

Examples:

- "I won't respond to personal messages during work hours."
- "I'm not available for late-night emotional conversations."
- "I won't make this decision for you."

If the boundary sounds like a suggestion, it isn't a boundary.

Avoid:

- "I'll try to…"

- "Maybe we could..."
- "I just need you to understand..."

C — Consequence (what *you* will do)

This step is often missed or misunderstood. Setting boundaries is not a process of telling other people how they should or are allowed to behave. Other people's behavior is outside of your control. Instead, setting boundaries is about changing how you react when faced with certain behaviors. Thus, the consequence phase is arguably the most important. When faced with dependent behavior, how will you react differently? How will you work to reset the system?

A consequence is not a punishment or a threat.

It simply describes **your response** if the boundary is crossed.

Examples:

- "If texts continue during work hours, I'll respond after work."
- "If the conversation becomes heated, I'll pause it and revisit later."
- "If this keeps looping, I'll step away from the discussion."

Without consequences, boundaries are theoretical.

Consequences make structure real.

The DESC framework in action

Here is what DESC looks like when integrated naturally into conversation:

"When you interrupt me during work hours with repeated messages (D), I feel distracted and overwhelmed (E). I'm not going to respond to personal texts while I'm working (S). If it continues, I'll reply after work instead (C)."

Notice what is absent:

- No over-explaining
- No defensiveness

- No negotiation
- Empathy paired with non-negotiability

It's clear and kind.

Why DESC works in dependent dynamics

DESC is particularly effective in dependent relationships because it:

- Limits emotional sprawl
- Reduces looping
- Protects conviction under pressure
- Prevents over-talking

DESC protects conviction by keeping communication structured rather than reactive. It gives you a **map** to return to when the conversation starts drifting.

When you repeat your DESC statements calmly, escalation loses traction. Consistency is more regulating than reassurance.

A grounding reminder

DESC is not about winning conversations.

It is about ending confusion.

You are not trying to convince someone to agree with your boundary.

You are informing them of how you will operate.

That distinction changes everything.

Section 7: Texting Undermines Conviction

Once boundaries are clear and communication is structured, there is one place where even the most confident people quietly lose ground.

Texting

Text feels efficient. It feels non-confrontational. It feels easier than talking in real time. For people who feel anxious about conflict, it can seem like the safest option.

In dependent dynamics, it is often the most destabilizing one.

Why text fuels dependency

Text removes the very elements that help regulate emotion:

- Tone
- Timing
- Containment
- Closure

Without those cues, messages are interpreted through anxiety. Pauses feel like rejection. Short responses feel cold. Long explanations invite negotiation.

Text allows conversations to stretch indefinitely without a clear beginning or end. It turns boundaries into ongoing threads instead of contained exchanges.

This is why dependent dynamics often intensify over text.

The illusion of control

Many people use text because they believe it gives them more control.

They can choose their words carefully. They can avoid confrontation. They can respond when they feel ready.

In practice, text often creates the opposite effect.

Because there is no clear endpoint, the conversation never fully stops. The phone becomes a portal to constant renegotiation. Each message invites another. Each pause invites anxiety.

Conviction erodes slowly, one reply at a time. Avoid having conversations about your boundaries over text.

When text is especially risky

Text is most destabilizing when:

- Boundaries are new
- Emotions are high
- Conversations tend to loop
- The other person seeks reassurance

In these moments, text amplifies uncertainty instead of resolving it.

Redirecting from text to containment

One of the most important skills to learn is how to redirect a text conversation without being pulled in.

Examples:

- "This isn't something I want to handle over text."
- "Let's talk about this later."
- "I'm not available to go back and forth right now."

Once you redirect, stop engaging.
Do not explain why.
Do not answer follow-up questions.
Do not soften the boundary.

Using text to reinforce, not renegotiate

Text is best used to **reinforce** boundaries, not negotiate them.

Appropriate uses:

- Restating a boundary already discussed
- Communicating logistics

- Confirming timing

Examples:

- "As I said before, I'm not available during work hours."
- "We'll talk tomorrow."
- "I'm logging off now."

Short. Predictable. Closed-ended.

What to avoid over text

Avoid:

- Emotional processing
- Justifying decisions
- Responding to accusations
- Reopening settled conversations

Text is not a neutral medium. It invites continuation.

If something matters, contain it.

Section 8: Ending Conversations Without Ghosting

When conversations become overwhelming, many people reach for the same escape.

They disappear.

They stop responding. They delay replies indefinitely. They hope the other person will "get the hint" and back off on their own.

This behavior often gets mislabeled as boundaries.

It isn't.

Ghosting is not boundary-setting.

It is avoidance.

And while it may bring temporary relief, it quietly undermines both people.

Why disappearing feels easier than speaking

Ghosting is usually not about indifference.

It is about fear.

Fear of confrontation.

Fear of hurting someone.

Fear of being seen as cruel.

Fear of triggering escalation.

For people who struggle with asserting limits, disappearing feels safer than being clear. It allows them to avoid the emotional discomfort of saying no while still reclaiming space.

The problem is that silence without structure creates confusion, not closure.

The cost of avoidance

When you disappear without explanation, the other person is left to fill in the gaps.

In dependent dynamics, those gaps are filled with anxiety, self-blame, and escalation. The nervous system searches harder for contact. The urge to re-engage intensifies.

Meanwhile, the person who disappeared often carries unresolved guilt.

They know they avoided a necessary conversation. They may feel relieved and ashamed at the same time. That emotional residue makes future boundary-setting even harder.

Avoidance postpones discomfort. Setting real boundaries will resolve it.

Clean endings are an act of maturity

Ending a conversation or relationship cleanly requires honesty and maturity.

Clean endings:

- State the decision
- Acknowledge emotion
- Do not invite negotiation

They are brief. They are clear. They are complete.

Examples:

- "I don't want to continue this relationship."
- "This dynamic isn't working for me."
- "I'm stepping back from contact."

These statements may feel blunt, but they are not unkind.

Ambiguity is far more destabilizing than unhappy news communicated clearly.

Why clarity is kinder than silence

Many people worry that stating an ending directly will cause pain.

Silence causes pain too. It just spreads it out and deepens it.

Clarity allows grief to begin. Silence keeps hope alive and prolongs distress.

You are not responsible for preventing someone else's feelings.

You are responsible for being honest about your limits.

Pairing empathy with non-negotiability

A clean ending can still include care.

Examples:

- "I know this is painful, and I'm still making this choice."
- "I care about you, and I'm not continuing this relationship."
- "This isn't easy for me, and it's not changing."

Notice what these statements do:

- They acknowledge emotion

- They state a decision
- They do not invite debate

The trap of leaving the door open

Many people soften endings by leaving the door open "just in case."

They say:

- "Maybe in the future..."
- "I just need some space right now..."
- "Let's see how things go..."

In dependent dynamics, this prolongs attachment and increases distress.

If the decision is to end contact, clarity is more humane than hope.

When the urge to ghost is a signal

If you feel a strong urge to disappear, pause.

Ask yourself:

- "What am I avoiding saying?"
- "What boundary am I afraid to state?"
- "What discomfort am I trying to escape?"

The urge to ghost often points directly to the boundary that needs to be communicated.

A grounding truth

Disappearing is not strength.

You can end conversations.

You can end relationships.

You can reclaim space.

And you can do so without cruelty, punishment, or collapse.

Section 9: Two Conversations, Two Outcomes

Up to this point, we have talked about communication in principles, patterns, and tools.

This section is where those ideas meet reality.

Because the difference between collapse and stability is rarely about what you understand or intend. Execution and action are critical.

I want to walk you through two conversations drawn from the kinds of cases you've already encountered in this book. I hope they will show how small communication shifts radically change outcomes.

Case One: When clarity exists but communication collapses

Jason had already reached a point of clarity.

He knew the relationship was unsustainable. He knew his constant reassurance and availability were fueling the problem rather than fixing it. He had even said, out loud, that he needed boundaries.

He had the insight. But it wasn't enough.

Here is how one of their conversations typically unfolded.

His partner would text repeatedly while he was at work:

"I don't feel okay."

"Are you mad at me?"

"Can you just tell me you're not leaving?"

Jason would feel the familiar surge of guilt. He knew responding immediately reinforced the pattern, but the distress felt urgent. He would answer:

"I'm not mad. I just have a lot going on."

"I care about you. I just need you to understand where I'm coming from."

That response opened the door.

She replied with more emotion, more urgency, more explanation requests. Jason stayed in the conversation longer than he meant to. He reassured. He clarified. He softened.

By the end, he felt drained and resentful. She felt temporarily soothed, but no more secure.

Nothing had changed.

His words kept shifting. His tone changed under pressure. The conversation never closed cleanly. Conviction eroded one sentence at a time.

Case Two: The same boundary, communicated differently

Contrast that with a later conversation after Jason learned to change how he communicated.

The same text arrived during work hours:

"I'm really anxious. Can you talk?"

This time, Jason paused.

He didn't disappear. He didn't explain. He didn't reassure.

He responded:

"I hear that you're anxious. I'm not available during work hours. We can talk later."

She pushed back:

"But I really need you right now."

Jason repeated himself, calmly:

"I know this feels urgent. I'm still not available. We'll talk later."

And then he stopped responding.

That was the entire exchange.

It wasn't dramatic. It wasn't cruel. It wasn't perfect.

But it was consistent.

Later that evening, when they spoke in person, the intensity was lower. The conversation was shorter. Jason felt steadier. His partner was still uncomfortable, but she had survived the discomfort without rescue.

The system shifted.

A second case: When boundaries create growth

Now contrast Jason's experience with the patient from Chapter 6, the man whose life had narrowed under the weight of his girlfriend's dependency.

Early on, his communication mirrored Jason's. He over-explained. He stayed engaged late into the night. He responded reflexively to distress.

Eventually, exhaustion forced a change.

Here is how one of his later conversations sounded.

When his girlfriend became distressed late at night, he said:

> "I care about you, and I'm not available for emotional conversations this late. We'll talk tomorrow."

She cried. She accused him of not caring. She escalated.

He stayed calm and repeated:

> "I'm still holding the boundary."

Then he ended the conversation and went to bed.

The next day was uncomfortable. But over time, something important happened.

Without constant nighttime regulation, she began seeking other supports. Not perfectly. Not immediately. But genuinely.

The relationship did not collapse.

It recalibrated.

What these conversations teach

In both cases, the boundary itself was the same.

What changed was the communication.

When communication was driven by guilt, fear, or urgency, the system stayed stuck.

When communication was driven by clarity and structure, the system adapted.

The uncomfortable truth

Boundaries do not work because they are fair.

They work because they are consistent.

When your words match your actions, over time, the relationship reveals whether it can adjust.

That information is invaluable.

A final reflection for this section

If you see yourself in these conversations, it does not mean you have failed.

It means you have been trying to hold structure without support.

The next section will turn this into something you can carry with you: a simple checklist that keeps communication grounded when pressure rises.

Section 10: A Personal Anchor — Learning to Say Less and Mean It

There is a reason this chapter matters to me beyond my clinical work.

Long before I understood dependent dynamics in patients, I lived a version of them myself.

In middle school, more than anything else, I wanted to belong. I wanted friends. I wanted acceptance. And I believed, without realizing it, that the way to earn that was to accommodate everyone.

I said yes to things I didn't want to do.

I laughed when I felt uncomfortable.

I adjusted myself constantly to avoid conflict or disapproval.

I talked more than I needed to. I explained myself when no explanation was required. I tried to be understood instead of being clear.

And the result was not closeness.

It was the opposite.

The more I bent, the less I was respected. The more I tried to manage how others felt about me, the less grounded I felt in myself. Eventually, I found myself with very few real connections and a growing sense that something was wrong with me.

What I didn't understand then was this:

People don't feel safer around someone who is endlessly accommodating. They feel safer around someone who is consistent.

That shift didn't happen overnight. It happened later, gradually, when I stopped trying to earn connection through explanation and started showing up with clearer edges.

I said less.

I stopped justifying.

I let some conversations end without resolution.

And something surprising happened.

People began gravitating toward me—not because I was louder or more persuasive but because I was steadier. My presence became more predictable. My words matched my actions.

That experience stayed with me.

Years later, in clinical settings, I began seeing the same pattern play out in far more complex ways. Different relationships. Higher stakes. More pain. But the same underlying dynamic.

People who believed they had to keep talking to stay connected.

People who feared that stopping meant abandoning.

People who thought clarity was cruelty.

Then, and now, the lesson has been the same:

You don't preserve connection by dissolving yourself into it.

You preserve connection by being clear enough to remain intact.

This chapter is not asking you to become less caring.

It is asking you to stop disappearing in the name of care.

Section 11: The Communication Checklist (and a Steady Close)

This checklist is designed to be another tool to help you stay grounded when communication becomes emotionally charged.

Because when pressure rises, it can undermine your ability to build new habits and maintain your boundaries.

This checklist is not about sounding polished. It is about protecting conviction when old reflexes resurface.

Use it before conversations that feel predictable, emotionally loaded, or destabilizing. Not in the middle of them.

The Communication Checklist

Before the conversation

- Am I clear about my boundary?
- Am I entering this as a decision or a dialogue?
- What emotion am I most likely to feel when this gets uncomfortable?

During the conversation

- Am I stating, or am I persuading?
- Am I saying more because it helps, or because I feel guilty?
- Is my tone warm *and* my boundary non-negotiable?

When emotion escalates

- Can I validate without surrendering structure?
- Am I staying anchored, or am I absorbing?
- Do I need to pause, close, or defer this conversation?

If the boundary is tested

- Have I already been clear?
- Am I repeating myself calmly?
- Are my words matching my decision?

When the conversation ends

- Did I stop cleanly, or did I trail off?
- Did I leave clarity, or ambiguity?
- What do I need to do now to regulate myself?

What to say less of

- Explanations that reopen settled decisions
- Apologies for having limits
- Emotional reassurance that substitutes for structure
- Arguments meant to be "understood"

What to say more of

- Clear, simple statements
- Calm repetition
- Acknowledgment of feeling without negotiation
- Clean endings

Transition to Chapter 8

In this chapter, we focused on **how to communicate boundaries once they exist**.

In the next chapter, we will address something just as important and often misunderstood: **what happens when communication alone isn't enough**.

Because sometimes, even the clearest boundaries and the steadiest communication do not lead to change.

Chapter 8 will explore **detachment, consequences, and what it means to step back without abandoning yourself or the other person**.

CHAPTER 8

When Communication Isn't Enough

Section 1

There is a moment in many relationships when the problem is no longer *how* something is being said.

By the time people reach this point, they have usually done everything they were told to do. They have clarified boundaries. They have softened their tone. They have validated feelings. They have used scripts, reflected emotions, and tried to stay calm under pressure. They have explained themselves carefully and repeatedly, hoping that the right combination of words might finally make something click.

And yet, nothing fundamentally changes.

This is not because communication does not matter. It is because communication has limits.

Clear communication can create understanding. It can reduce confusion. It can prevent unnecessary conflict. What it cannot do is compel responsibility or growth in someone who is not ready or able to take it.

In my clinical experience, this is one of the most painful realizations for people in dependent dynamics. They often assume that if the relationship is still strained, they must be saying or doing something wrong. They revisit the conversation in their minds, replaying each word, wondering if they sounded too firm, too soft, too emotional, or not emotional enough.

This self-interrogation becomes its own trap.

When understanding is present, but behavior does not change, communication is no longer the problem. Structure is.

For some relationships, clarity lands, and the system adapts. Boundaries are tested, then respected. Roles rebalance. Growth happens slowly, imperfectly, but genuinely.

For others, clarity changes very little.

The dependent person may nod in agreement. They may repeat back what you have said. They may even show brief improvement. But the pattern reasserts itself. The same requests return. The same crises emerge. The same expectations resurface, as if the conversation never happened.

This does not mean you failed. It means you reached the edge of what words can do. What you can do.

One of the most common forms of false hope in dependent relationships is the belief that insight will inevitably lead to change. People cling to moments of apparent understanding as proof that they just need to hold on a little longer, explain a little better, or be a little more patient.

But understanding can coexist with avoidance. Agreement can coexist with dependency. Saying "I get it" is not the same as doing something differently when it matters.

This is where many people feel disoriented. They have done everything "right," and yet the weight of the relationship remains on their shoulders. They feel guilty for wanting to escalate, even though nothing else has worked. They worry that stepping back means giving up, being cold, or abandoning someone who needs them.

This chapter exists for that moment.

Detachment is not introduced because communication was insufficiently compassionate or precise. It is introduced because, at some point, communication alone stops moving the system forward. Setting your boundaries isn't creating behavioral change.

Repeated patterns tell you something important about capacity. Not about intent, not about goodness, but about what the relationship can currently sustain. When behavior does not change despite clearly communicated boundaries, the system is communicating back to you, whether you want to hear it or not.

What it is saying is this: words are no longer enough.

Detachment is not the opposite of communication. It is what follows when communication has reached its limit.

For some people, this realization brings relief. For others, it brings grief. Often, it brings both at the same time.

Relief, because they finally understand why nothing they say seems to land.

Grief, because it means accepting that love and effort alone cannot carry the relationship forward.

This is a difficult threshold to cross. Many people linger here for months or years, hoping that one more conversation will be the one that finally shifts everything. But hope that delays necessary change eventually becomes another form of self-erasure.

Stepping into detachment does not mean abandoning care. It means acknowledging reality.

And acknowledging reality is often the most compassionate act available.

Section 2: What Detachment Is — and What It Is Not

Detachment is one of the most misunderstood concepts in behavioral health and that misunderstanding is the reason many people resist it long after it becomes necessary.

For many readers, the word itself triggers alarm. It sounds cold. Final. Punitive. Like a door closing or a relationship being downgraded. People imagine emotional withdrawal, silent treatment, or indifference disguised as self-care.

That is not what detachment means in this book.

Detachment is not abandonment, rejection, or punishment. It's not about giving up on someone.

Detachment is regulated distance.

It is the intentional creation of space so that a relationship can recalibrate instead of collapsing under strain. It is stepping back *with awareness*, not disappearing out of fear or exhaustion. It is choosing structure over reactivity, and sustainability over short-term relief.

In my clinical experience, people most often confuse detachment with emotional cruelty because they associate love with constant engagement. If you have spent years equating care with availability, any reduction in access can feel like harm, even when that access is costing you your stability.

Detachment challenges that equation.

It introduces a different definition of love, one that does not require you to absorb every consequence of someone else's choices.

This distinction matters because many people delay detachment because they are afraid of what detachment *means* about them. They worry it signals failure, selfishness, or moral weakness. They worry it proves they did not love enough.

In reality, detachment often becomes necessary *because* you have loved deeply and tried everything else.

Detachment is not permanent separation.

It is not divorce by another name.

It is not moving across the country or blocking someone on your phone.

For some people, detachment may be temporary. For others, it may be ongoing. But its purpose is not to sever connection but to create conditions under which the connection can continue in a safe, healthy, sustainable way.

When a relationship becomes organized around dependency, one person's nervous system becomes the stabilizer for both. Detachment interrupts that pattern. It returns regulation, responsibility, and agency to where they belong.

This is why detachment often feels more threatening than boundaries or communication. Boundaries tell someone what you will or will not do. Communication clarifies how you will speak and engage. Detachment changes *access*.

Access is powerful.

Access determines who absorbs distress, who solves problems, and who pays the emotional cost of repeated patterns. When you step back, even slightly, the system feels it immediately.

For some people, that is when growth begins.

For others, it is when resistance intensifies.

Detachment does not guarantee improvement. What it guarantees is honesty. It shows you, and the other person, what happens when the relationship is no longer cushioned by your constant intervention.

That is why detachment is not something we force.

We do not detach to scare someone into changing. We do not detach to "teach them a lesson." We do not detach to gain leverage.

Detachment is a response to information.

It comes after boundaries have been stated.

After communication has been clarified.

After understanding has been demonstrated without sustained change.

At that point, continuing to engage in the same way is not kindness. It is maintenance of a system that no longer works.

For some people, detachment is an act of respect.

It says, *I trust you enough to tolerate discomfort without me rescuing you.*

It says, *I will not infantilize you by preventing every consequence.*

It says, *I value this relationship enough to stop enabling what is harming it.*

This is why detachment is not the same as indifference.

Indifference disengages emotionally and morally. Detachment stays emotionally regulated while changing behavior. Indifference says, *I don't care what happens.* Detachment says, *I care enough to stop participating in something unsustainable.*

There is also an important distinction between detachment and neglect.

Detachment involves clear communication, predictable structure, and continued concern for safety. Neglect is withdrawal without clarity, support, or accountability. Detachment creates space *with intention.* Neglect disappears without explanation.

In this chapter, we are staying firmly on the side of detachment.

You remain emotionally available, but not endlessly accessible.

You remain caring, but not controlling.

You remain present, but not responsible for outcomes that are not yours to manage.

For some readers, this reframing alone will feel relieving. For others, it will feel unsettling. That discomfort does not mean detachment is wrong. It means it is unfamiliar.

If you have spent years stabilizing someone else's emotional world, stepping back will feel risky, even dangerous. Your nervous system has learned that proximity equals safety.

Detachment asks you to learn something new: that distance, when regulated and intentional, can also be safe.

And sometimes, it is the only thing that allows a relationship to survive at all.

In the next section, we will move from philosophy to mechanics. We will look closely at **consequences**, not as punishment or cruelty, but as information, and why allowing consequences is often the turning point when nothing else has worked.

Section 3: Consequences – Information, Not Punishment

This is the heart of detachment, and it is where many people get stuck.

Even when someone understands boundaries and communication, consequences often feel like crossing a moral line. They sound harsh. Final. Vindictive. People worry that allowing consequences means they are being cruel, cold, or intentionally hurtful.

In my clinical experience, this fear is one of the strongest barriers to change.

So we need to be precise about what consequences are, and just as importantly, what they are not.

A consequence is a natural or logical outcome of a choice or behavior.

That is all it is.

A consequence is not something you *do to* someone. It is something that *happens when a choice is made.* It is connected to behavior, predictable, and ideally communicated in advance. Its purpose is not to cause pain, but to create understanding.

Consequences provide information.

They answer a simple question: *What happens if this continues?*

In dependent dynamics, that information is often missing, because someone else absorbs the impact. You smooth things over. You rescue. You compensate. You intervene before the system can respond.

Over time, this creates a distorted reality. The dependent person does not experience the full weight of their choices because someone else is carrying that weight for them.

Detachment restores accuracy.

A useful way to understand this is to contrast consequences with punishment.

Punishment is imposed. It is emotional. It is often driven by anger, frustration, or the desire to control behavior. Punishment is frequently disproportionate or unrelated to the original action. Its message is, *I'm making you suffer because you did something wrong.*

Consequences, by contrast, are proportional and connected. Their message is simpler: *This is what happens when this choice is made.*

For example:

- Miss a deadline, and the project moves forward without your input.
- Spend the money, and it is no longer available later.
- Yell at someone, and they disengage or end the conversation.
- Skip therapy sessions, and progress stalls.

None of these are punishments. They are realities.

In dependent relationships, people often try to eliminate consequences in the name of compassion. They step in early. They soften outcomes. They provide endless second chances. They do this because watching someone struggle is uncomfortable.

But removing consequences does not reduce suffering in the long run. It redistributes it.

You feel it instead.

This is where detachment becomes an ethical act.

When you allow consequences to occur, you are not harming the other person. You are refusing to shield them from reality. You are allowing learning, responsibility, and agency to emerge. You are creating conditions for growth.

This is why I say clearly and without apology: you are not responsible for protecting someone from the consequences of their choices.

That does not mean you stop caring. It means you stop over-functioning.

In my clinical work, I often see people confuse kindness with protection. They believe that if they care enough, they can prevent pain. But pain that is prevented too early often returns later in more destructive forms.

Consider a simple example.

A partner says, "If you call me repeatedly during meetings, I won't respond until after the weekend." The boundary is clear. The consequence is predictable. The behavior continues anyway.

When the partner follows through and does not respond until Monday, they are not being cruel. They are being consistent. They are protecting their time and attention.

The dependent person may feel distressed. They may feel anxious. That discomfort is not the result of punishment. It is the result of behavior meeting reality.

For some people, this is the first time the dots connect.

Consequences only work when they are:

- Directly linked to the behavior
- Proportionate
- Predictable
- Non-emotional
- Followed through consistently

Once consequences are allowed, ambiguity disappears. The system can no longer pretend that nothing happens when boundaries are ignored.

This is why consequences often feel like a turning point. They mark the shift from endless discussion to lived experience.

That shift is uncomfortable. It can provoke backlash, guilt, and fear. But it is also where change becomes possible.

In the next section, we will look at how to recognize when communication is no longer the problem, and when detachment and consequences are no longer optional, but necessary.

Section 4: When Clarity Doesn't Change Behavior

One of the hardest truths for people to accept is this: **clear communication does not guarantee change.**

This is not a failure of empathy. It is not a failure of wording. And it is not a failure of effort.

It is a reality-based observation.

Most people assume that if they explain themselves well enough, the other person will eventually respond differently. They believe that understanding naturally leads to action. When that does not happen, they turn inward and assume they must be doing something wrong.

In my clinical experience, this assumption keeps people stuck far longer than necessary.

There is an important difference between *not understanding* and *not changing.*

Someone may genuinely understand your boundary and still not be able or willing to behave differently. They may repeat your words back to you accurately. They may agree with you intellectually. They may even feel remorse in the moment.

And yet, the pattern continues.

This is the point where many people get confused. They say things like:

- "They really do get it."
- "They say all the right things."
- "They promised it would be different."
- "They seemed sincere."

Sincerity is not the same as capacity.

Understanding is not the same as follow-through.

When behavior does not change despite repeated clarity, the issue is no longer communication. The issue is accountability and structure.

There are a few signs that signal this shift clearly.

The first is **temporary improvement followed by regression**.
After a serious conversation, things improve for a short time. You feel hopeful. You relax. Then, gradually, the old behaviors return. Often quietly. Often framed as exceptions. Often justified by stress, circumstances, or emotion.

The second is **repeated promises without durable change**.
You hear apologies. You hear insight. You hear commitments. What you do not see is sustained behavior that holds when it is inconvenient.

The third is **escalation when boundaries are enforced**.
When you follow through on a limit, the response intensifies. Emotions spike. Accusations appear. The conversation shifts away from behavior and toward your tone, your timing, or your character.

The fourth is **blame directed at the communication itself**.
Instead of addressing the behavior, the focus becomes how you said it. You are told you were too harsh, too calm, too distant, too emotional. The boundary becomes the problem, not the pattern that required it.

For some people, one of these signs is enough. For others, it is the accumulation that makes it undeniable.

This is where detachment becomes relevant.

Words alone do not produce movement.

For some people, stepping back feels like admitting defeat. They worry that they are "giving up" too soon. But detachment is not about giving up. It is about stopping a strategy that is no longer working.

Continuing to communicate without changing structure often reinforces dependency. It teaches the other person that insight is sufficient, that apologies reset the system, and that consequences never truly arrive.

Detachment interrupts that loop.

It introduces a different kind of message. Not spoken but lived.

It says: understanding matters, but behavior matters more.

Detachment does not mean silence. It does not mean coldness. It does not mean disappearing.

It means accepting that communication has reached its limit and that responsibility cannot be carried for someone else any longer.

In the next section, we will look at what detachment actually looks like in real relationships, and how to step back without crossing into neglect or abandonment.

Section 5: What Detachment Looks Like in Real Life (And What It Doesn't)

Detachment often sounds abstract until people see it lived out.

That abstraction is part of why it feels frightening. When people hear the word *detachment*, they imagine extremes. Silence. Withdrawal. Cold distance. Cutting someone off without explanation. Emotional abandonment disguised as self-care.

That is not what we are talking about here.

Detachment, as we are using it in this book, is not disappearance. It is **regulated distance**.

In my clinical experience, detachment works best when it is **intentional, communicated, and proportionate**. It is not impulsive. It is not retaliatory. And it is not meant to shock someone into change.

Detachment is what happens when you stop compensating for behavior that has not changed, while remaining emotionally grounded and clear about why.

Let's be concrete.

Detachment often looks like:

- Reducing frequency of contact after repeated boundary violations

- Limiting emotional availability when conversations become circular or dysregulated
- Allowing someone to feel frustration, disappointment, or anxiety without intervening
- Following through on previously stated consequences
- Stepping back from roles you quietly assumed but never agreed to carry indefinitely

What detachment does **not** look like:

- Silent treatment
- Ghosting
- Sudden emotional coldness
- Withholding affection to punish
- Creating distance without explanation

Detachment is not meant to confuse or destabilize the other person. It is meant to restore balance to a system that has become distorted.

For some people, detachment will be subtle. For others, it will feel dramatic simply because the system has relied so heavily on your over-functioning. The intensity of the reaction does not determine whether the step is appropriate.

For example, a parent with an adult child who calls multiple times a day may move to scheduled check-ins instead of constant availability. A partner who has repeatedly explained a boundary around work interruptions may stop responding during work hours altogether. A loved one who has been providing constant emotional reassurance may step back and redirect the person toward other supports.

None of these are punishments. They are recalibrations.

A useful way to think about detachment is this: **You are changing your participation, not trying to change them.**

That shift is crucial.

Detachment does not say, "You need to be different."

It says, "I am no longer going to participate in this pattern."

This is also where people worry about neglect.

Detachment becomes neglect when you withdraw from a role you still reasonably occupy *without communication or replacement support.* For example, disappearing from a child's life without explanation, abandoning someone in a true crisis, or stepping away from responsibilities without ensuring safety.

Detachment stays ethical when:

- The boundary is communicated clearly
- Safety is not compromised
- The distance is appropriate to the situation
- Emotional availability remains, even if access changes

You are not abandoning someone by refusing to absorb their anxiety. You are not neglecting them by allowing discomfort. You are not being cruel by stepping out of a role you never agreed to play indefinitely.

Detachment does not mean you stop caring. It means you stop carrying.

That difference may sound subtle, but it changes everything.

In the next section, we will walk through specific real-world scenarios where detachment and consequences become necessary, and how this looks across different relationships without crossing ethical lines.

Section 6: Allowing Consequences Without Cruelty

This is the point where detachment becomes real.

Up until now, many people can agree with the ideas in theory. They understand boundaries. They understand communication. They even understand detachment conceptually. What stops them is this moment right here.

The moment when they have to let something *happen*.

For many people, allowing consequences feels far more uncomfortable than continuing to rescue. Rescue is familiar. Rescue provides immediate relief. Rescue quiets guilt and restores a sense of control.

Consequences do none of those things at first.

In my clinical experience, this is where people hesitate the most, because consequences feel like an action of harm rather than an act of restraint. They worry they are being punitive. They worry they are being unloving. They worry they are intentionally letting someone suffer.

That is not what is happening.

Allowing consequences is not about making someone uncomfortable. It is about **no longer interfering with reality**.

When someone violates a boundary, and nothing changes, the system learns that boundaries are optional. When someone violates a boundary and experiences a predictable outcome, the system learns something new.

This is why consequences must be:

- Clearly connected to the behavior
- Communicated in advance when possible
- Proportionate
- Non-emotional
- Followed through consistently

Consistency is the part most people underestimate.

For some people, a consequence only needs to happen once for the message to land. For others, it needs to happen repeatedly before the pattern shifts. What matters is not how quickly the other person changes, but whether *you* remain aligned with what you said you would do.

Let's return to an earlier example.

A partner says, "If you call repeatedly during my meetings, I won't respond until after work." The calls continue. The response does not.

This is not silent treatment. It is follow-through.

A parent says, "If you don't attend class consistently, I won't step in to fix the consequences with your school." The behavior continues. The parent steps back.

This is not abandonment. It is responsibility returning to where it belongs.

A loved one says, "If conversations escalate into yelling, I will end the conversation." The yelling happens. The conversation ends.

This is not coldness. It is structure.

What makes these moments hard is not the consequence itself, but what you have to tolerate emotionally while it unfolds. You may witness distress, anger, panic, or blame. You may be accused of being uncaring. You may feel a surge of guilt that tells you to intervene.

That guilt is familiar. It is also misleading.

For many people, guilt arises not because they are doing harm, but because they are no longer playing the role that kept the system stable. The discomfort you feel is often the same discomfort the other person is feeling, mirrored back to you.

Allowing consequences requires you to tolerate that discomfort without converting it into action.

This is not easy. It is a skill.

It may help to remember this: **rescuing feels kind in the moment, but it delays learning**.

When consequences are consistently allowed, the other person gains access to information they have not had before. They see the connection between their choices and their outcomes. They experience agency even if that agency initially feels uncomfortable.

This does not guarantee change. Nothing does.

But without consequences, change is almost impossible.

One of the most common fears people express is, "What if this makes things worse?"

Sometimes, things do get worse before they get better. Distress often increases when old coping strategies stop working. This does not mean the consequence was wrong. It means the system is adjusting.

For some people, consequences lead to growth. For others, they reveal limits. Either way, they clarify reality.

And clarity, even when painful, is kinder than endless confusion.

In the next section, we will look at specific relationship scenarios where detachment and consequences are most commonly needed, and how to navigate them without crossing into neglect or cruelty.

Section 7: Common Scenarios Where Detachment Becomes Necessary

Detachment usually does not arrive all at once. It emerges after repeated attempts to communicate, clarify, and set boundaries have failed to produce lasting change. In my clinical experience, there are several situations where this shift becomes particularly necessary. These examples are not prescriptions. They are illustrations. For some people, detachment helps restore balance. For others, it reveals limits that communication alone could not clarify.

1. **The Partner Who Refuses Responsibility**

   For some partners, dependency shows up as chronic avoidance of responsibility. They may understand your boundaries intellectually. They may agree with them. They may even express remorse. But behavior does not change in durable ways.

   You may hear:

   - "I know, I know. You're right."
   - "I didn't mean to do it again."
   - "I'll try harder."

   And yet, the same behaviors continue.

In these situations, continued discussion often becomes performative. The dependent partner learns that insight resets the system, even when action does not follow. Detachment here often means stepping back from compensating for the fallout of their choices.

For some people, this looks like no longer fixing missed deadlines, no longer smoothing over social consequences, or no longer absorbing emotional outbursts. It is not punitive. It is proportional. It allows responsibility to land where it belongs.

2. The Adult Child Who Will Not Launch

This is one of the most emotionally complex scenarios.

Parents often fear that detachment will feel like abandonment, especially when an adult child struggles with anxiety, immaturity, or avoidance. Many parents tell themselves that stepping in is temporary. That their child just needs a little more time.

Years can pass this way.

In my clinical experience, growth often begins only after access changes. Scheduled check-ins replace constant contact. Parents stop intervening in academic, financial, or interpersonal problems. Discomfort rises. So does guilt.

For some families, this space allows the adult child to develop the competence they never had to access before. For others, it reveals the need for additional support outside the parent-child dyad.

Detachment here is not about withdrawing love. It is about restoring developmental balance.

3. The Parent Who Demands Continued Caretaking

Sometimes the dependency flows in the opposite direction.

An aging or emotionally dependent parent may rely heavily on an adult child for regulation, reassurance, or decision-making. Requests are framed as needs. Guilt is used, often unintentionally, to maintain closeness.

In these cases, detachment often means limiting availability, redefining roles, and allowing the parent to tolerate frustration or loneliness without immediate rescue.

For some people, this step is accompanied by grief. The fantasy of a mutually supportive relationship has to be revised. Detachment allows reality to replace obligation.

4. The Loved One with Addiction or Emotional Dysregulation

This is perhaps the most misunderstood scenario.

For some people struggling with substance use or severe emotional dysregulation, communication and boundaries alone are insufficient. Continued rescue delays change. Natural consequences, while painful, often create the conditions for insight.

In addiction work, we often see that meaningful change begins only after consequences accumulate. Jobs are lost. Relationships fracture. Supports are withdrawn.

This is not cruelty. It is reality.

Detachment here must always be paired with safety considerations and professional support. But shielding someone from consequences indefinitely does not protect them. It prevents growth.

Across all of these scenarios, the common thread is this: detachment becomes necessary when your involvement is the only thing keeping the system afloat.

Stepping back does not guarantee a positive outcome. It does, however, guarantee clarity.

In the next section, we will look at the emotional barriers that make detachment so difficult to sustain, and how to tolerate the discomfort without retreating.

Section 8: The Emotional Barriers That Make Detachment So Hard

Even when people understand detachment intellectually, following through can feel unbearable.

The difficulty is not logistical. It is emotional.

In my clinical experience, most people do not abandon detachment because they doubt its logic. They abandon it because of what it asks them to tolerate internally. The emotions that surface during detachment are often intense, confusing, and morally charged.

The most common barrier is **guilt**.

Guilt tells you that if someone is suffering, you must be at fault. It whispers that love requires intervention, that stepping back is the same as not caring, and that allowing discomfort is a personal failure. For people who have spent years regulating others, guilt feels familiar and convincing.

But guilt is not always a moral signal. In dependent systems, guilt is often a conditioned response. It arises because the role you have been playing is changing, not because you are doing something wrong.

Another powerful barrier is **pity**.

Pity often disguises itself as compassion. You see the dependent person's distress and imagine how hard things must feel for them. You tell yourself they are fragile, overwhelmed, or incapable of handling what you are asking. You rationalize stepping back as something they simply cannot tolerate.

What pity does, unintentionally, is freeze someone in that role.

When we act from pity, we lower expectations. We assume incapacity. We remove opportunities for growth before they are even attempted.

Hope can also keep people stuck.

Hope sounds virtuous. It feels generous. But hope that repeatedly overrides evidence becomes avoidance. People tell themselves that things are improving because they want to believe it. They cling to moments of progress while minimizing the larger pattern of regression.

Hope without structure often delays necessary change.

Fear is another quiet driver.

Fear of conflict. Fear of escalation. Fear of being seen as cold. Fear of what might happen if you are no longer the one holding everything together.

For some people, fear is tied to identity. They have built a sense of self around being the reliable one, the strong one, the rescuer. Detachment threatens that identity. It asks, Who are you if you are no longer needed in the same way?

There is also **grief**.

Even when detachment is healthy, it often involves mourning the relationship you hoped for. The version where communication alone would be enough. The version where effort was reciprocated. The version where love did not require so much structure.

This grief is usually quiet and unacknowledged. People rush past it, focusing on logistics and boundaries, without allowing themselves to feel the loss.

Acknowledging grief does not mean giving up. It means making room for reality.

What all of these emotions have in common is that they pull you back toward familiar roles. They tempt you to intervene, explain, rescue, or soften consequences.

Detachment asks something different.

It asks you to tolerate discomfort without converting it into action. To allow emotions to rise and fall without making them directives. To trust that stepping back, even when it feels wrong, may be the most honest response available.

This is not easy work. It is not fast. And it is rarely clean.

But it is often what allows clarity, growth, or resolution to finally emerge.

In the next section, we will look at how to hold detachment ethically, especially in situations involving mental illness, addiction, or fragility, and where the line must be drawn to avoid neglect or harm.

Section 9: Ethical Lines — Detachment, Neglect, and Endangerment

Detachment must be held within clear ethical boundaries.

This is especially important in relationships involving mental illness, addiction, or significant emotional fragility. Without clarity, people either detach too little and remain trapped, or detach too abruptly and cause harm.

So we need to be explicit about the differences.

Detachment is regulated distance.

Neglect is withdrawal without responsibility.

Endangerment is withdrawal that places someone at risk.

These are not interchangeable.

In my clinical experience, people who are afraid of detachment often imagine neglect or endangerment, even when what they are proposing is neither. That fear keeps them over-involved far longer than is healthy.

Let's ground this with an example.

Consider a parent with an adult son who is dependent.

> **Appropriate detachment** looks like allowing the son to experience frustration, failure, or discomfort without intervening, while remaining emotionally available and ensuring safety. The parent communicates clearly, adjusts access intentionally, and encourages outside support.

> **Neglect** occurs when a parent withdraws from a role they still reasonably occupy without communication or replacement support. For example, disappearing emotionally, refusing all contact without explanation, or stepping away from responsibilities that cannot ethically be abandoned.

Endangerment occurs when withdrawal places someone at risk. This includes ignoring credible threats of self-harm, medical emergencies, or legal danger, or removing support without ensuring safety nets are in place.

The key difference between detachment and neglect is **intentionality and communication**.

Detachment is named. It is explained. It is held consistently. It does not disappear without warning. It does not pretend the relationship no longer exists.

Neglect avoids. It disappears. It abdicates responsibility without acknowledgment.

Another important distinction is **capacity**.

Detachment assumes the other person has some capacity to tolerate discomfort, even if it is difficult. Endangerment ignores situations where capacity is genuinely compromised.

This is why detachment should never override safety. If someone is at immediate risk to themselves or others, boundaries pause. Help is mobilized. Detachment resumes only after safety is restored.

This is not inconsistency. It is ethics.

Many people fear that once they step back, they will slide into cruelty or abandonment. In reality, most people who worry about this are highly conscientious. They are not trying to escape responsibility. They are trying to hold it without being consumed by it.

Ethical detachment requires ongoing self-checks:

- Am I stepping back to protect sustainability, not to punish?
- Is safety intact?
- Is the boundary communicated and proportional?
- Am I allowing discomfort, not danger?

When these conditions are met, detachment is not abandonment. It is stewardship.

In the final section, we will bring this chapter to a close with a quiet, grounding permission — not to disengage impulsively, but to trust yourself when communication and boundaries have reached their limit.

Section 10: A Quiet Permission to Step Back

If you have made it this far into the chapter, you have likely reached a difficult internal crossroads.

You understand boundaries.

You have learned how to communicate without collapsing.

You have tried clarity, consistency, empathy, and follow-through.

And now you are here, facing the possibility that stepping back may be the most honest next step.

Many people wait for permission to do this. Not explicit permission from the other person, but moral permission. A sense that they are not doing something wrong, cruel, or selfish by changing how they participate.

So let me offer that permission plainly.

You are allowed to step back.

You are allowed to stop intervening when intervention has become the only thing holding the system together. You are allowed to let discomfort exist without rushing to eliminate it. You are allowed to trust what repeated patterns have already shown you.

Detachment is not something you do because you have run out of compassion. It is something you do because compassion without structure has stopped working.

For some people, detachment becomes a bridge. Space allows recalibration. Roles shift. Responsibility redistributes. The relationship finds a new, healthier shape.

For others, detachment becomes information. It reveals limits. It clarifies capacity. It shows you what is possible and what is not.

Both outcomes are valuable.

What detachment gives you, above all, is truth.

Truth about what you can sustain.

Truth about what the relationship can tolerate.

Truth about whether change is possible without you carrying everything alone.

This truth can be uncomfortable. It can bring grief. It can bring relief. Often, it brings both at the same time.

If part of you is still asking, *What if I'm wrong?*

That question does not mean you should stay stuck.

It means you care.

Caring does not require self-sacrifice.

Love does not require endless rescue.

Growth does not happen when reality is softened beyond recognition.

You are not stepping back to hurt someone.

You are stepping back to stop harming yourself.

And sometimes, those two things are inseparable.

In the next chapter, we will turn toward what happens after detachment begins — how relationships either reorganize, stabilize, or reach their natural endpoint, and how to navigate that next phase with clarity rather than fear.

For now, let this be enough:

You are not cruel for stepping back.

You are not failing for letting consequences speak.

You are allowed to choose sustainability over survival.

That choice is not abandonment.

It is adulthood.

Section 11: A Simple Consequence Check-In

Before you step back, it helps to pause.

Not to second-guess yourself, but to make sure your detachment is intentional rather than reactive. This brief check-in is not a test. It is a way to ground yourself when emotions are loud and guilt is persuasive.

Use this when you feel pulled to intervene "one more time."

1. What behavior has not changed?

Be specific. Avoid global judgments.

Not:

"They never listen."

But:

"They continue to call repeatedly during work hours after I've been clear."

Clarity reduces self-doubt.

2. What have I already tried?

List it honestly:

- Clear boundaries
- Calm communication
- Empathy and validation
- Follow-through
- Time

Detachment is not the first move. It is what comes *after* effort.

3. What consequence naturally follows if I stop intervening?

This should be logical, not dramatic.

Examples:

- They feel anxious during the day
- They have to solve the problem themselves

- The conversation pauses
- Support shifts elsewhere

If the consequence feels punitive, reassess. If it feels neutral and connected, you're likely on solid ground.

4. Is safety intact?

Ask plainly:

- Is there immediate risk to life, health, or legal safety?
- Is this discomfort, not danger?

If safety is at risk, detachment pauses. Ethics come first.

5. What am I protecting by stepping back?

This question matters.

Not:
"What am I doing to them?"

But:
"What am I preserving in myself?"

Energy. Stability. Dignity. Sustainability.

Detachment held for self-protection is different from withdrawal fueled by anger.

6. What feeling am I tolerating instead of acting on?

Name it:

- Guilt
- Fear
- Pity
- Hope
- Responsibility

Feelings are allowed, but they are not instructions.

7. **What would happen if nothing changed for another year?**

This is not meant to scare you.

It is meant to clarify the costs of the status quo.

Staying is a choice. So is stepping back.

A final grounding reminder

You do not need to detach perfectly.

You do not need certainty.

You do not need permission from the person who benefits from things staying the same.

You only need honesty.

Detachment is not a statement about the other person's worth. It is a statement about what you can sustainably carry.

CHAPTER 9

Encouraging Independence

Section 1: What Happens After Detachment Begins

There is a moment after detachment when many people expect relief and instead feel unsettled.

They have done something difficult and necessary. They have stepped back. They have stopped rescuing, over-explaining, or absorbing consequences that were never meant to be theirs. Intellectually, they know they have crossed an important threshold.

Emotionally, however, things can feel surprisingly unstable.

In my clinical experience, this is one of the most confusing phases for people in dependent relationships. They often assume that detachment should immediately bring peace or clarity. When it does not, they begin to question themselves. They wonder if they moved too fast, if they were too firm, or if they misread the situation entirely. They worry they made a mistake.

This uncertainty is not a sign that detachment was wrong. It is a sign that the system is changing.

Detachment does not resolve dependency overnight. It disrupts it. And disruption, even when healthy, rarely feels calm at first.

For some people, the period after detachment is marked by turbulence. The dependent person may panic, escalate emotionally, or cycle through promises and distress. The reader may feel a strange mix of relief and guilt, steadiness and sadness, resolve and doubt. These opposing feelings often coexist in uncomfortable ways.

It is important to name this early: feeling unsettled after detachment does not mean you made a mistake. It means you are no longer cushioning a system that depended on your constant intervention.

Detachment removes a familiar stabilizer. For a long time, your availability may have been the emotional glue holding things together. When that glue is no longer applied, the relationship has to reorganize. That reorganization can feel chaotic before it becomes clearer.

Many readers reach this phase with a quiet hope that detachment will finally "fix" things. They imagine that once they step back, the dependent person will immediately rise to the occasion, take responsibility, and function independently. Sometimes that happens. More often, it does not happen quickly.

For some people, detachment reveals growth potential. Space allows them to tolerate discomfort, solve problems, and develop capacities that were never accessed before. For others, detachment reveals limits. Without rescue, they struggle, withdraw, or seek another source of regulation.

Neither outcome means you failed.

This distinction matters because many people interpret continued difficulty as proof that detachment was a mistake. They tell themselves that if things are still messy, they must go back in and help more. This impulse is understandable. It is also often the very thing that keeps dependency intact.

Detachment is not a magic solution. It's a process.

It provides information that communication alone cannot. It shows you what happens when responsibility is no longer shared unevenly. It clarifies whether independence can emerge, and if so, how slowly and under what conditions.

For some readers, this realization brings relief. They finally understand why no amount of explaining ever changed the dynamic. For others, it brings grief. They are forced to reckon with the possibility that the relationship they hoped for may not exist in the way they imagined.

Relief and grief often arrive together.

You may feel relieved that you are no longer carrying everything alone. You may also feel sad that it had to come to this. Both reactions are normal. Both deserve space.

It is also common during this phase to feel emotionally drained. Detachment requires restraint, and restraint takes energy. You may notice that you are less reactive, but more tired. Less entangled, but more reflective. This is not regression. It is recalibration.

In my clinical experience, people often underestimate how much adjustment detachment requires internally. You are not only changing how you relate to another person. You are changing how you respond to your own anxiety, guilt, and sense of responsibility. That shift takes time.

For some people, the turbulence after detachment lasts several weeks. For others, it stretches longer. What matters most is not how quickly things settle, but whether you resist the urge to undo the step you took simply because change feels uncomfortable.

This chapter is not about rushing independence or demanding outcomes. It is about understanding what typically unfolds after detachment begins, so you are not caught off guard by its emotional complexity and challenges.

Detachment is not the end of the work. It is the beginning of a different phase.

In the sections that follow, we will talk about how independence actually develops, why it cannot be forced, and how to recognize real growth when it appears. We will also address the grief, doubt, and hope that accompany this phase, so you are not navigating it alone or in silence.

For now, it is enough to know this: if things feel unsettled after detachment, you are not doing it wrong. You are standing in the middle of change.

And change, even when healthy, rarely feels tidy at first.

Section 2: What Independence Is — and What It Is Not

Independence is another word that carries far more emotional weight than people realize.

By the time readers reach this chapter, many of them already feel conflicted about the idea. They may want independence for the dependent person, but feel uneasy naming it directly. The word itself can sound harsh, as if it implies abandonment, impatience, or a demand that someone suddenly function in ways they never have before.

So we need to slow this down and be precise.

Independence does not mean throwing someone into the deep end and telling them to swim or drown.

It does not mean cutting them off emotionally, withdrawing love, or pretending their struggles are insignificant. It does not mean that you stop caring, stop worrying, or stop feeling connected.

And it is not a zero-sum game.

In healthy forms of independence, there are often two winners. You regain your freedom, stability, and sense of self while the other person gains access to capacities they couldn't develop while being rescued.

Independence, as we are using it in this book, means this:

It means a person is increasingly able to tolerate discomfort without outsourcing it.

It means they take responsibility for their own emotions, decisions, and consequences.

It means they can struggle, fail, adjust, and recover without someone else stepping in to regulate the experience for them.

This kind of independence does not arrive all at once. It develops gradually, unevenly, and often awkwardly.

One of the biggest misunderstandings in dependent dynamics is the belief that independence is something you demand or enforce. That if you just push hard enough, explain clearly enough, or step back decisively enough, the other person will "get it" and suddenly mature.

In my clinical experience, independence cannot be forced.

Pressure may produce compliance, but it rarely produces capacity. Fear may create temporary behavior change, but it does not build internal regulation or confidence. Growth that lasts almost always comes from experience, not instruction. This is why support and rescue must be distinguished.

Support says, "I believe you can handle this, even if it's uncomfortable."

Rescue says, "This is too much for you, so I'll take it over."

Support preserves independence while rescue quietly undermines it.

Many readers struggle here because they genuinely care about the dependent person and do not want to see them suffer. They may tell themselves that stepping in is kindness, that easing discomfort is compassion, that shielding someone from distress is loving.

But over time, repeated rescue sends an unintended message: *you cannot do this without me.*

That message, even when delivered gently, erodes independence.

Another common misunderstanding is the belief that independence requires emotional coldness. People worry that if they stop intervening, they will become distant, uncaring, or selfish. This fear is especially strong for those who have spent years measuring love by availability.

Independence does not require emotional withdrawal.

You can remain warm, caring, and emotionally present while no longer taking responsibility for what is not yours to carry. You can acknowledge struggle without fixing it. You can express belief in someone's ability without rushing to prove it for them.

This is also where readers often turn their judgment inward.

They criticize themselves for wanting space. They label themselves selfish or greedy for needing relief. They assume that asking for independence is a moral failure rather than a reasonable need.

That self-attack is part of the old system.

Just as the dependent person has to grow into greater autonomy, the non-dependent person has to grow out of over-responsibility. That growth involves tolerating anxiety, resisting rescue, and allowing space to exist even when it feels wrong at first.

Independence is not only something the dependent person develops. It is also something the reader must learn to allow.

And allowing independence often feels harder than enforcing closeness.

In the next section, we will look at what tends to happen after detachment. We will walk through the patterns, setbacks, and uneven progress that often emerge, so you are not mistaking turbulence for failure or struggle for regression.

Independence is rarely dramatic. It is usually quiet, slow, and imperfect.

And that is exactly how real growth tends to look.

Section 3: What Actually Happens After Detachment

Detachment does not create immediate stability. It creates movement.

That movement can look chaotic before it looks healthy.

For some people, the first response to detachment is escalation. Panic increases. Contact attempts multiply. Language becomes urgent, dramatic, or emotionally loaded. This is not a sign that detachment was wrong. It is often a sign that the old system no longer works.

When a dependent person loses immediate access to their regulator, their nervous system reacts. The behaviors that once restored relief no longer produce the same outcome. The system searches for its previous equilibrium.

This phase is uncomfortable for everyone involved.

For others, detachment triggers bargaining.

You may hear promises, sudden insight, or declarations of change. The dependent person may appear motivated, reflective, or unusually compliant. This can feel hopeful, and sometimes it is. Other times, it is an attempt to restore closeness without building capacity.

In my clinical experience, this phase often includes temporary improvement followed by regression.

Things look better for a short time. You relax slightly. Then, gradually, old patterns resurface. Not always in obvious ways. Often in subtler forms that are easier to rationalize.

This does not mean the effort was meaningless. Growth is rarely linear.

Another common response is withdrawal.

The dependent person may pull back emotionally. They may appear distant, flat, or disengaged. Some readers interpret this as progress. Others experience it as rejection or punishment. Often it's simply grief. Dependency does not disappear quietly. When old roles dissolve, there is often a period of mourning. The dependent person is losing access and identity. They are confronting the reality that something they relied on is no longer available in the same way.

This is where people often feel tempted to rush in and reassure.

They worry the withdrawal means harm. They worry they have gone too far. They worry the relationship is dying.

Sometimes a relationship *is* ending. But very often, this phase is transitional.

In many cases, genuine but uneven growth begins here.

The dependent person starts experimenting with new ways of coping. They tolerate discomfort for longer stretches. They delay outreach. They solve some problems independently while still struggling with others. Progress comes in bursts, not in a straight line.

This is also the stage where replacement dependencies may appear.

The dependent person may lean heavily on a new partner, therapist, friend, institution, or system. This can feel alarming to the reader, as if nothing has changed.

In my clinical experience, replacement dependencies are often weaker and shorter-lived than the original dynamic. They may serve as scaffolding while independence develops. Sometimes they dissolve on their own. Sometimes they reveal areas where additional support is still needed.

Struggle during this phase is expected.

What's important is that you resist the urge to re-enter the role of primary regulator when struggle occurs.

This phase typically lasts weeks, not days.

For some people, the most turbulent period spans eight to twelve weeks. Around the fourth week, many readers report something important: they can finally breathe. The constant vigilance decreases. The anticipatory anxiety softens. The relationship no longer consumes their inner world in the same way.

This does not mean everything is resolved.

It means the system is reorganizing.

It is crucial not to mistake turbulence for failure.

Detachment is not meant to eliminate discomfort. It is meant to relocate it. Instead of one person absorbing all of it, discomfort becomes distributed more accurately across the system.

That redistribution is what creates the conditions for independence.

After detachment, the goal is not to punish or be punitive. It is to prioritize yourself and create space for something new to develop, whether that is growth, clarity, or closure.

In the next section, we will look at how to tell the difference between real independence emerging and dependency simply changing its form, so you are not pulled back in by appearances alone.

Sections 4 and 5: How to Tell When Independence Is Real (and When It Isn't)

One of the hardest tasks after detachment is not stepping back.

It is deciding when, and how, to step forward again.

Most readers are not afraid of independence. They are afraid of being fooled by something that looks like progress but collapses the moment pressure returns. After months or years of carrying the relationship, it makes sense that you want reassurance before you re-engage.

But real independence rarely announces itself dramatically. It reveals itself quietly, through behavior that holds under stress. It's demonstrated slowly over time.

What you are looking for is not perfection.

You are looking for patterns.

A simple way to stay oriented is to think in three categories: green flags, yellow flags, and red flags.

Green Flags: Signs Independence Is Actually Developing

Green flags are behavioral, not verbal.

1) **Delayed outreach**

Instead of reaching out immediately at the first sign of discomfort, the dependent person pauses. They tolerate uncertainty longer. They attempt something on their own before seeking support.

When they do reach out, the tone shifts.

Less urgency. Less crisis language. More curiosity.

You may hear:

- "I wasn't sure what to do, so I tried a few things first."
- "I handled most of it, but I could use perspective."
- "I want to talk this through, not because I'm falling apart, but because I'm thinking."

2) **Self-initiated problem solving**

They take steps without being prompted. They make decisions, tolerate mistakes, and recover without demanding immediate reassurance. Help is sought after effort, not before it.

3) **Reduced emotional intensity**

The same stressors that once triggered spirals now produce more contained reactions. Frustration still exists, but it is not treated as an emergency that must be outsourced.

4) **Accountability without defensiveness**

When something goes poorly, they are less likely to externalize blame. They may still struggle, but they begin owning their role in outcomes and focusing on what they can do differently next time.

5) **Progress that exists when you are not watching**

This matters more than people realize.

Independence is not performative. It does not require an audience. If the only progress happens when you are present, involved, or monitoring, it is not yet stable.

Yellow Flags: What Looks Promising but Often Isn't (Yet)

Yellow flags are signs of change, evidence of a transitional phase. They suggest potential, but more work is still needed.

1) Insight without action

The dependent person can articulate the problem clearly. They may even use language that sounds emotionally sophisticated. But behavior does not consistently change.

This does not always mean manipulation. It often means understanding has arrived faster than capacity.

2) Short-lived compliance

After detachment, there may be a burst of improvement. Boundaries are respected. Communication improves. You feel hopeful.

Then, after days or weeks, old patterns return in quieter forms.

In many cases, effort is real, but tolerance is still fragile. The intention is there. The skill is not consolidated yet.

3) Emotional speeches

Heartfelt conversations about growth, remorse, gratitude, or fear of loss can feel deeply sincere.

But emotional expression is not the same as behavioral change.

Sometimes emotional depth becomes a substitute for responsibility. A moving conversation temporarily restores closeness without building capacity.

How to respond to yellow flags

Yellow flags are signals to slow down, not to rush back in, and not to disappear completely.

They mean: keep the structure, watch the pattern, and let time do some of the work.

Red Flags: When Dependency Is Still Running the System

Red flags suggest that rescue is still expected and that the system is still organized around you as the regulator.

1) Blame and responsibility shifting

When discomfort arises, the problem is framed as your fault.

"This is happening because you changed."

"If you were more supportive, I wouldn't be like this."

"You're the reason this is so hard."

There's a strong emotional reaction AND a refusal to take responsibility.

2) Escalation when structure holds

Anger, rage, threats, dramatic emotional swings, or punishment show up when boundaries remain in place.

Sometimes this reflects grief. Sometimes it reflects limited capacity. Either way, it is information: the person is not tolerating independence.

3) Manipulation and guilt-tripping

Statements that frame you as cruel, selfish, or abandoning are attempts to restore the old emotional contract.

They may not be conscious. They are still powerful.

4) Boundary testing and "exceptions"

Limits are pushed subtly or repeatedly, often framed as misunderstandings or special cases. The focus is not on adapting to structure, but on finding ways around it.

5) Dependency disguised as closeness

This is one of the most confusing ones.

The language may sound healthy: connection, teamwork, "we're doing so much better."

But if closeness still requires you to regulate, reassure, fix, or absorb distress, the function has not changed.

6) Replacement dependency that is intense and rigid

Not all outside support is bad. In fact, it is often helpful.

But swapping one rescuer for another without increased autonomy can delay growth. If the new support becomes exclusive, urgent, or compulsory, it may be dependency wearing different clothes.

How to Use These Signals Without Becoming Hypervigilant

These categories are not meant to turn you into a monitor.

In my clinical experience, people who have carried too much responsibility often swing from over-involvement to over-analysis. That is not the goal.

You do not need to track every behavior. You do not need to interrogate every conversation.

What matters is pattern, not perfection.

- **Green flags** show up consistently over time, including under stress.
- **Yellow flags** fluctuate, improve briefly, regress, then improve again.
- **Red flags** persist and intensify when structure is maintained.

When independence begins to emerge, re-engagement works best when it is **slow and incremental** with guardrails in place.

Access increases gradually. Support is offered **after effort**, not before. Consequences are not undone retroactively.

If outside support is present (therapy, coaching, structured accountability), re-engagement becomes safer because you are no longer the sole stabilizing force.

Everything will not suddenly feel easy, but responsibility should begin to shift back where it belongs.

And the most reliable proof is not a promise.

It is steadiness.

Section 6: Common Dependency Responses When Independence Begins

When independence starts to emerge, it often destabilizes the dependent system before it stabilizes it.

For some people, the loss of immediate access to reassurance, regulation, or rescue creates a surge of emotional responses. These reactions are not necessarily signs of malice or manipulation. In many cases, they are expressions of grief, fear, and uncertainty as old roles dissolve.

Understanding these responses in advance helps you hold your position without becoming reactive or punitive.

Bargaining

For some people, independence attempts trigger bargaining.

This often sounds like:

"If you just do this one thing, I'll be okay."

"Can we go back to how things were, just a little?"

"I promise this time will be different."

Bargaining is an attempt to restore closeness without building capacity. It is not always conscious. It reflects fear more than defiance.

In my clinical experience, engaging with bargaining pulls readers back into negotiation rather than structure. The conversation shifts from responsibility to reassurance, and the boundary quietly erodes.

Responding with empathy while maintaining distance sounds like: "I hear how hard this is. The structure we set is still important."

Victim Language

Another common response is victim language.

"You're abandoning me."

"You're giving up on me."

"I can't believe you'd do this after everything."

This language is powerful because it activates guilt and responsibility. It reframes independence as harm and detachment as betrayal.

For some people, this reflects genuine fear of being alone. For others, it reflects an attempt to reassert the old emotional contract.

In either case, it functions to try to reestablish the dependent relationship.

Acknowledging the feeling without accepting the premise is key: "I know this feels scary. Stepping back doesn't mean I don't care."

Blame-Shifting

Blame-shifting often follows when victim language fails.

"This is happening because you changed."

"If you were more patient, I wouldn't be like this."

"You're the reason this is so hard."

This response externalizes responsibility and undermines conviction. It pressures the reader to justify themselves instead of staying grounded in structure.

In my clinical experience, engaging with blame-shifting leads to circular conversations that exhaust both people and delay growth.

A steady response does not argue facts. It returns to reality: "I'm not going to debate this. The structure remains."

Crisis Inflation

When independence threatens the system, every problem may suddenly feel urgent.

Minor stressors escalate into emergencies. The tone becomes dramatic. The request for help becomes immediate.

But urgency does not equal danger.

When every situation is framed as a crisis, independence cannot develop. The nervous system never learns to tolerate uncertainty.

Holding structure here is essential. You can acknowledge distress without responding as if catastrophe is imminent.

Anger, Threats, or Escalation

Some people respond to independence with anger.

They raise their voice. They issue threats. They accuse. They escalate.

This often reflects grief and loss of control rather than true hostility. Still, it is a signal that the person is not yet able to engage safely.

In these moments, detachment must remain firm. Escalation is not a reason to re-engage more deeply. It is information.

Silent Treatment or Withdrawal

Withdrawal can look like progress, but it is not always.

The dependent person may pull away emotionally, stop communicating, or become cold. For readers, this can feel punishing or frightening.

In my clinical experience, withdrawal is often part of mourning. It does not necessarily mean independence is failing. It means the person is recalibrating.

The key question is whether withdrawal leads to reflection and growth, or whether it becomes a new way to exert pressure.

Recruiting Allies

One of the most destabilizing responses is recruiting others.

"They agree you're wrong."

"Everyone thinks you're being cruel."

"My therapist says you're the problem."

This tactic widens the emotional field and increases self-doubt. It is designed, consciously or not, to override your conviction through social pressure.

When this happens, return to your original clarity. The presence of allies does not change the reality of the pattern.

Why recognizing these responses matters

These reactions do not mean independence is failing. They mean the system is changing.

For some people, these responses soften over time. For others, they reveal limits that were previously hidden by rescue and reassurance.

Your job is not to diagnose, fix, or confront these responses.

Your job is to notice them, stay grounded, and avoid stepping back into the role that made them necessary in the first place.

In the next section, we will focus on how to encourage independence without cruelty — how to validate effort, maintain compassion, and support growth without undoing the very conditions that allow it to happen.

Section 7: Encouraging Independence Without Cruelty

Once detachment is in place and consequences are allowed, many readers ask the same question:

If I'm not rescuing, what am I supposed to do instead?

This is an important question because independence does not develop in a vacuum. It develops in a relational field that is structured, predictable, and emotionally regulated.

Independence develops most reliably when three conditions are present: belief, restraint, and consistency.

Belief: Communicating confidence without control

For some people, the most powerful intervention is not what you *do*, but what you communicate implicitly.

When you step back without panic, over-explaining, or constant monitoring, you send a quiet but important message: *I believe you can handle this.*

This belief does not need to be argued or proven. In fact, the more you try to persuade someone of your confidence in them, the more it can sound like reassurance rather than conviction.

Belief shows up as steadiness.

It sounds like:

"I trust you to figure this out."

"I'm here to talk about it later, not to take it over."

"I know this is uncomfortable, and I believe you can tolerate it."

Belief does **not** sound like cheerleading, pressure, or conditional approval. It is not, "You've got this, don't mess it up." It is not, "I'll help if you try harder."

It is quiet confidence that does not rush to fill the silence.

Restraint: Letting effort precede support

One of the hardest shifts for readers is learning to let effort come *before* support.

In dependent dynamics, support often arrives preemptively. You step in at the first sign of struggle. You offer solutions before effort has even begun. You try to prevent discomfort rather than allow it.

Encouraging independence requires restraint.

Restraint means pausing before helping. It means asking, "What have you tried?" instead of "Here's what you should do."

It means allowing small failures to occur without immediately repairing them.

You allow learning to happen through experience, not explanation.

Consistency: Supporting growth without resetting the system

Encouragement only works if the structure remains intact.

One of the most confusing experiences for a dependent person is inconsistent re-engagement. When access expands and contracts unpredictably, the system never stabilizes. Independence cannot develop in moving goalposts.

You don't need to be rigid but you do need to be predictable.

If contact is scheduled, it stays scheduled.

If responsibility has shifted, it stays shifted.

If consequences were allowed, they are not undone retroactively.

When progress appears, re-engagement should be **slow and incremental**, with clear guardrails in place.

For example:

- Increased contact may come with maintained boundaries
- Emotional availability may increase without resuming rescue
- Support may be offered after effort, not before

This pacing matters.

Moving too quickly back into closeness often reactivates dependency before independence has had time to consolidate.

Validating effort without managing outcomes

Encouraging independence does not mean evaluating or grading someone's performance.

It means noticing effort without taking ownership of results.

Validation sounds like:

"I see that you tried something new."

"I know that wasn't easy."

"I can imagine that felt uncomfortable."

Validation does *not* sound like:

"I'm proud of you for doing it the right way."

"You should have done it differently."

"At least you didn't mess it up."

When validation turns into assessment, it quietly reintroduces hierarchy. Independence requires dignity, not supervision.

Giving permission not to rush growth

Many readers need explicit permission to slow down.

Independence does not develop on your timeline. It unfolds unevenly with advances and setbacks. Trying to accelerate it often recreates pressure and fear, which are states that undermine growth.

In my clinical work, I often say this directly:

> You are allowed to let growth be slow.
>
> You are allowed to tolerate awkwardness.
>
> You are allowed to stop monitoring progress constantly.

Encouragement works best when it is patient and non-performative.

What encouragement is not

It may help to be clear about what encouraging independence is *not.*

It is not motivating speeches.

It is not repeated reminders.

It is not warnings about what will happen if they fail.

It is not rescuing disguised as support.

Encouragement is not something you do *to* someone. It is something you create space *for.*

When belief, restraint, and consistency are present, independence has room to develop. When they are absent, even the best intentions can collapse back into dependency.

In the final section, we will close this chapter by turning inward, helping the reader tolerate the slower pace of change, the emotional ambiguity of growth, and the quiet grief that often accompanies letting go of old roles.

Section 8: Letting Independence Unfold

By the time you reach this point, something important has already happened.

You have stopped trying to force outcomes.

You have stopped believing that love means constant intervention.

You have accepted that growth, when it comes, comes slowly.

That is a profound shift.

For many readers, this phase feels strangely empty at first. The urgency has eased, but so has the sense of purpose that came from being needed. The constant motion of rescuing, fixing, anticipating, and managing is gone. In its place, there is space.

That space can feel peaceful, but it can also feel unsettling.

This is often where grief shows up quietly.

The soft grief of releasing a role you once believed defined the relationship or even your identity. You may find yourself mourning the version of connection you hoped would exist, the version where care flowed without cost, where effort was reciprocated, where love did not require so much structure.

Even when independence is developing, there is loss.

It is possible to feel relieved and sad at the same time.

It is possible to feel proud and unsure.

It is possible to care deeply and still step back.

None of these feelings mean you are doing something wrong.

Letting independence unfold means resisting the urge to monitor every outcome. It means allowing periods of silence without filling them. It means trusting that not everything meaningful needs to be visible or immediate.

Growth is rarely loud.

It is often subtle, uneven, and easy to miss if you are watching too closely.

You may notice that your own nervous system begins to settle in new ways. The anticipatory anxiety softens. The urge to check, intervene, or brace decreases. Your attention returns to parts of your life that were previously overshadowed. You are slowly recalibrating.

You are not withdrawing love.

You are withdrawing over-functioning.

Independence, when it develops, does not always look like confidence or success. Sometimes it looks like persistence. Sometimes it looks like failure followed by trying again. Sometimes it looks like silence that is no longer filled with panic.

Your role now is not to supervise this process.

It is to tolerate it.

To tolerate not knowing exactly how things will turn out.

To tolerate discomfort without converting it into action.

To tolerate the possibility that the relationship may change in ways you did not anticipate.

This tolerance is not passive.

It is an active choice to stop carrying what is not yours.

If part of you still wonders whether stepping back makes you cold, remind yourself of this:

You did not stop caring.
You stopped compensating.

You did not abandon.
You allowed room.

You did not fail.
You responded honestly to what the relationship required.

Independence cannot be forced.
But it can be invited.

And sometimes, the most powerful invitation is simply making space and trusting that whatever grows there will be more real than what was held together by rescue alone.

In the next chapter, we will turn toward what happens as relationships either stabilize, reorganize, or reach their natural endpoint, and how to navigate that phase with clarity rather than fear.

For now, let this be enough.

You are allowed to step back.

You are allowed to let growth be slow.

You are allowed to choose sustainability over sacrifice.

Section 9: Staying Oriented as Independence Grows

After detachment and the early phases of independence, many readers expect certainty.

They want to know:

Is this working?

Am I doing the right thing?

Should I step back more, or re-engage now?

This desire for certainty is understandable. For a long time, you were the stabilizer. You were used to tracking the emotional weather of the relationship and adjusting yourself accordingly. Letting go of that role often leaves people feeling unmoored, even when things are objectively healthier.

This section is not about giving you new rules. It is about helping you stay oriented.

A simple independence check-in

When doubt creeps in, return to these questions. Not to interrogate yourself, but to ground yourself.

1. **Is the relationship less urgent than it used to be?**
   Even if it is not yet calm, is it less frantic? Less consuming? Less organized around crisis?

   Urgency decreasing is often one of the earliest signs that independence is taking hold.

2. **Am I doing less emotional labor than before?**
   Are you explaining less, fixing less, anticipating less? Are you spending less time bracing for reactions?

   Your relief matters.

3. Is effort coming from them before it comes from me?

It does not need to be perfect. It does not need to be consistent yet. But is there any evidence of self-initiated action?

4. Am I holding structure without resentment?

Resentment often signals over-functioning. Calm firmness often signals alignment.

If you are able to hold boundaries without simmering anger, you are likely in the right place.

5. Have I stopped trying to manage the outcome?

Independence develops best when you are no longer monitoring it like a performance review. If you can tolerate not knowing exactly how this ends, you have already loosened the old grip.

A final orientation

Encouraging independence is not about creating distance forever. It is about creating the conditions for a different kind of closeness, one that does not rely on rescue, panic, or imbalance.

Whether the relationship ultimately stabilizes, reorganizes, or ends, the work you are doing now matters.

You are learning to:

- Let responsibility land where it belongs
- Allow discomfort without converting it into action
- Stay connected without disappearing
- Trust reality instead of managing perception

If you find yourself wondering whether you have done enough, remember this:

You did not force change.

You did not abandon care.

You did not act out of anger or fear.

You responded thoughtfully to what the relationship required.

And whatever happens next, you are no longer building connections on self-sacrifice alone.

That is real progress.

Section 10: A Quiet Permission to Let Independence Unfold

At this point in the journey, many readers expect a final instruction.

They look for a rule, a test, or a guarantee. Something that tells them whether they are doing this "right," or how long they must hold steady before things feel settled.

There is no such rule.

Independence does not unfold on a clean timeline. It does not move in straight lines. And it does not arrive with certainty attached.

What you are doing now is not managing an outcome.

You are creating conditions.

You have stepped back without disappearing.

You have allowed discomfort without cruelty.

You have stopped rescuing without withdrawing love.

That is already enough.

For some people, the dependent person will continue to grow. Slowly. Unevenly. Sometimes frustratingly. But with real shifts that become more consistent over time.

For others, independence will reveal limits. The relationship may not reorganize in the way you hoped. There may be grief in that realization, even if it is also clarifying.

Both outcomes are honest.

What matters is that you are no longer contorting yourself to keep something alive at your own expense. You are no longer confusing endurance with love. You are no longer using proximity as proof of care. You have learned to tolerate the space where growth happens.

If part of you still feels sad that does not mean you are doing this wrong. It means you are human. Loss and progress often coexist. Relief and grief are not opposites. They frequently arrive together.

You are allowed to miss what was, even if what was was unsustainable.

You are allowed to care, even as you stop carrying.

You are allowed to step back without needing to justify it to the person who benefited most from things staying the same.

Independence is not something you demand.

It is something you allow.

And allowing it requires patience, restraint, and trust in reality rather than fantasy.

If you are wondering what to do next, let this be enough for now:

Hold the structure.

Stay regulated.

Let time and behavior speak.

You have already done the hardest part.

In the next chapter, we will turn toward what happens when independence stabilizes — how relationships either settle into a healthier form, reach a natural conclusion, or require a different kind of letting go. For now, you are exactly where you need to be.

Not because everything is resolved.

But because you are no longer lost inside it.

CHAPTER 10

Love and Obligation

Section 1–2: Love vs. Obligation

There comes a point in many dependent relationships when something feels off, but it is difficult to name.

On the surface, everything still looks like care. You show up. You help. You give. You stay. From the outside, it may even look admirable. You are loyal. You are committed. You are not abandoning someone who needs you.

But internally, something has shifted.

The giving no longer feels light. The helping no longer feels generous. What once may have felt chosen now feels required. And yet, instead of questioning the dynamic, many people do something else. They tell themselves this is love.

In my clinical experience, this is one of the most painful and confusing traps people fall into. Not because they lack insight, but because obligation and love can feel almost identical when guilt is involved. The mind has a way of softening the truth when the truth feels too threatening to hold.

This chapter is about slowing that moment down.

It is about helping you tell the difference between what you genuinely want to give and what you feel coerced into giving. Between care that expands you and care that quietly erases you. Between love that is chosen and obligation that is rationalized.

This is not a chapter about becoming cold, detached, or selfish. And it is not an argument for abandoning commitment or responsibility. It is an invitation to look honestly at the internal experience of giving, rather than the moral story you have been telling yourself about it.

Because the body knows before the mind does.

Many readers arrive at this chapter feeling emotionally exhausted but morally trapped. They know something is wrong, yet they cannot justify stopping. When they imagine pulling back, guilt floods in. When they imagine continuing, resentment simmers. They feel caught between being a "good" person and being a whole person.

For some people, this conflict is intensified by culture.

In many Latino, South Asian, Middle Eastern, and collectivist cultures, love and obligation are deeply intertwined. Caretaking is often framed as virtue. Sacrifice is normalized. Loyalty to family and elders is not optional. In those contexts, questioning obligation can feel like questioning identity, values, and belonging all at once.

This chapter does not ask you to reject your culture or betray your values.

It asks you to locate yourself within them.

You are allowed to define what love feels like in your body, even within strong cultural expectations. You are allowed to notice when giving feels nourishing and when it feels coercive. And you are allowed to hold both truths without shame.

Before we go any further, we need to define what we mean by "love" and by "obligation".

Obligation is driven by duty, fear, and "shoulds."

Love is driven by desire, connection, and choice.

Obligation feels heavy. Love feels expansive.

Obligation says, "I have to do this."

Love says, "I want to do this."

When obligation is absent, people feel guilt or fear of consequences.

When love is absent, people feel sadness or longing.

Here is the distinction more clearly:

Love

- Primary driver: Desire and connection
- Internal feeling: Warmth, fulfillment, aliveness
- The "why": I want to do this for you
- Result if absent: Sadness, missing, grief

Obligation

- Primary driver: Duty, pressure, fear
- Internal feeling: Weight, resentment, fatigue
- The "why": I have to do this for you
- Result if absent: Guilt, anxiety, fear of backlash

This distinction matters because many people call obligation by kinder names.

They call it loyalty or commitment.

They call it being a good partner, child, or sibling.

They call it "not abandoning someone."

"Not abandoning someone" is the most common disguise obligation wears. Once the primary reason you are giving is because someone needs you, would fall apart without you, or could not cope if you stopped, the dynamic has shifted.

A useful internal test is this: If this were someone else, would I still do this?

Loyalty, commitment, and doing the right thing tend to pass that test. They are values that apply across relationships. Obligation often does not.

It is person-specific, fear-based, and anchored to consequences rather than desire.

Another way to tell is to listen to the body.

Obligation does not usually feel dramatic at first. It is subtle. A low-grade tension. A constant readiness. A background hum of anxiety and resentment that builds slowly over time. Many people describe it as a simmering pressure, like something always needs to be managed.

Not acting brings guilt and shame.

Acting brings resentment and a sense of coercion.

You may notice yourself bracing before interactions. Taking a deep breath before answering the phone. Feeling your chest tighten when you see their name on your screen. Mentally rehearsing how to help without getting angry, or how to say yes without feeling trapped.

That is not love.

Love, when obligation is removed, often feels quieter than people expect. It is not always dramatic or sacrificial. It can feel joyful, even selfish, in a healthy way. There is pleasure in giving. A sense of choice. A dopamine-like satisfaction that comes from wanting to show up, not needing to.

People sometimes feel almost indebted in love, but not because they are pressured. Because they genuinely want to give back. The giving feels voluntary, alive, and self-reinforcing.

So why do these two experiences get so tangled?

Because obligation is painful to acknowledge.

The mind often re-labels obligation as love to protect you from guilt, grief, and moral injury. Calling it love makes the sacrifice feel meaningful. It makes the exhaustion feel noble. It justifies staying in situations that are quietly draining you.

Once love and obligation become enmeshed, it becomes difficult to separate them without discomfort. Untangling them forces questions many people have avoided for years.

Am I still choosing this? Do I actually want to be here?

If guilt were removed, what would I do?

For many readers, these questions feel dangerous. They fear that asking them means they are heartless, selfish, or ungrateful. They fear what it would say about them if the answer is not what it "should" be.

This is where cultural messaging, moral identity, and fear of guilt converge. People stay not because they believe it will eventually pay off, but because the cost of guilt feels unbearable. They would rather endure resentment than face the idea that choosing themselves might make them a bad person.

This chapter is not here to push you toward leaving, detaching, or staying.

It is here to help you regain choice.

Love should be conditional. Not transactional, but contingent on mutual respect, emotional nourishment, and sustainability. Love that requires self-erasure is not love. Care that destroys you is not virtue. If it costs you your identity, it is no longer love. You can love deeply and still step back. You can care and still set limits. You can honor your values without becoming a slave to them.

This chapter hopes to help you see clearly. To recognize when your mind is rationalizing obligation as love. To notice what your body has been signaling for a long time. And to give you permission to question exhaustion without having to justify it.

In the sections that follow, we will look at why obligation is so hard to release, how guilt distorts decision-making, and how to test internally whether what you are sustaining is love or coercion.

For now, let this land gently.

You are not cruel for asking these questions.

You are not immoral for feeling tired.

And wanting your care to feel chosen does not make you unloving.

It makes you honest.

Many people understand this distinction intellectually, but struggle to feel it. Sometimes it helps to see the difference laid out plainly.

Feature	Love	Obligation
Primary Driver	Desire and connection.	Duty and "shoulds."
Internal Feeling	Lightness, warmth, or fulfillment.	Weight, resentment, or fatigue.
The "Why"	"I want to do this for you."	"I have to do this for you."
Result of Absence	Sadness or longing.	Guilt or fear of consequences.

Section 3: Why Obligation Feels Like Love (and Why It's So Hard to Let Go)

If obligation feels so heavy and love feels so different, a natural question follows:

> Why do so many intelligent, self-aware people confuse the two for so long?

Obligation hurts to name.

It carries grief, guilt, and the terrifying implication that something you believed was loving may be unsustainable. When the psyche senses that kind of threat, it often reaches for a softer explanation. One that preserves meaning and minimizes pain.

That explanation is love.

The mind has a remarkable ability to reframe distressing realities in ways that allow us to keep going. When giving becomes exhausting, when resentment creeps in, when anxiety replaces warmth, the mind often does not say, "This is costing me too much."

Instead, it says, "This is what love looks like."

This reframing reduces cognitive dissonance. It protects moral identity. It allows you to continue functioning without confronting loss or making disruptive changes. And for a time, it works.

But it comes at a cost.

Once obligation is labeled as love, the two become fused. Any attempt to pull back no longer feels like a practical adjustment. It feels like a failure. Saying no does not feel like boundary-setting. It feels cruel. Exhaustion does not feel like a signal. It feels like weakness.

This fusion is one of the main reasons people stay in obligation-based dynamics far longer than they should.

Guilt plays a central role here.

Many readers tell me some version of this:

"I don't even know if I want this anymore, but I'd feel terrible if I stopped."

That sentence contains the entire problem.

The motivation is no longer desire, connection, or joy. It is avoidance of guilt.

Fear compounds this further.

People fear being seen as selfish. They fear disappointing family. They fear violating cultural or moral norms. They fear becoming someone they do not recognize. And perhaps most powerfully, they fear the idea that if they stop, the other person will fall apart.

In my clinical experience, this fear is almost always exaggerated.

People are far more resilient than we imagine them to be. The belief that "everything will collapse without me" is usually a reflection of anticipatory anxiety, not reality. Yet that belief feels convincing because it has been rehearsed internally for years.

Obligation also makes seductive promises.

It promises that if you endure long enough, things will eventually change.

It promises that your sacrifice will be recognized or repaid.

It promises that staying proves you are loving, loyal, and good.

These promises rarely materialize.

What usually happens instead is quiet erosion. The resentment grows. Emotional availability shrinks. Intimacy suffers. And the version of you that once gave freely becomes harder to access, not just in this relationship, but in others as well.

Another reason obligation feels like love is that it often begins during legitimate hardship.

Illness. Addiction. Trauma. Loss. A period when one person genuinely needs more support.

At first, the giving is appropriate and compassionate. But over time, the dependent person stops contributing. Responsibility consolidates on one side. The dynamic becomes asymmetrical.

The person carrying more often interprets this as strength.

"I'm the strong one."

"I can handle it."

"They need me more than I need them."

In reality, strength is not the issue. Balance is.

What looks like strength is often just one person continuing to function while the other withdraws from responsibility. The scale tips, and obligation quietly replaces reciprocity.

Letting go of obligation is hard because it requires mourning.

You are not just releasing a behavior. You are grieving an image of yourself as endlessly giving, morally upright, indispensable. You are also grieving the relationship you hoped would exist if you had just given a little more.

Many readers resist this grief by doubling down on sacrifice. They tell themselves that the discomfort is proof they are doing the right thing. That if it hurts, it must be meaningful.

But pain alone does not confer virtue. Endurance is not devotion.

What makes obligation particularly sticky is that it masquerades as morality. It frames itself as selflessness, even as it drains your capacity to care. It convinces you that leaving or detaching would make you a worse person, even as staying makes you smaller.

This is why simply telling someone to "set boundaries" is rarely enough.

Until love and obligation are separated internally, any boundary will feel like betrayal. Any pause will feel like abandonment. Any attempt to choose yourself will feel like harm.

This chapter is not asking you to make a decision yet.

It is asking you to notice.

Notice when your reasons for giving are rooted in fear rather than desire.

Notice when guilt, not connection, is doing the motivational work.

Notice when the story of love is being used to anesthetize resentment.

These observations are not accusations. They are information.

In the next section, we will begin to look at how to tell when independence and genuine love are emerging, and when dependency is simply changing form. We will give you clearer internal markers so you are no longer relying on moral pressure to guide deeply personal decisions.

For now, let this be enough:

If love feels like captivity, it's not love.

If giving feels compulsory, it's not giving.

Noticing these truths does not make you heartless.

Section 4: Love Without Self-Erasure

One of the most frightening questions readers encounter at this stage is not whether they are exhausted.

It is whether choosing themselves means they are no longer loving.

For people who have spent years giving, accommodating, stabilizing, and absorbing, love has often been defined by endurance. By staying. By tolerating. By continuing even when something inside has gone quiet or numb.

So when the idea of stepping back arises, it can feel like a moral rupture.

"If I stop doing this, what does that say about me?"

"If I still love them, shouldn't I be able to keep going?"

"If I choose myself, am I choosing against love?"

These questions are not signs of selfishness. They are signs that love has been fused with self-erasure.

In my clinical experience, many people have never been taught that love and disappearance are not the same thing.

They have learned, implicitly or explicitly, that care requires sacrifice. That being good means being available. That leaving room for yourself means taking something away from others.

But love that requires you to erase yourself is not sustainable love.

It may begin with generosity, but over time it becomes depletion.

It is important to say this clearly, without harshness:

It is possible to love someone deeply and still step back.
It is possible to care and still detach.
It is possible to hold warmth without holding responsibility that is not yours.

What often gets mislabeled as love in dependent dynamics is actually fear-based attachment.

Fear of being seen as abandoning.

Fear of causing pain.

Fear of violating identity.

Fear of becoming "the bad one."

Love, by contrast, does not require constant self-negation.

Love allows movement.

Love allows differentiation.

Love allows both people to exist fully, not just one.

This is where many readers confuse love with self-sacrifice.

Self-sacrifice is giving that leaves you emptier every time.

Love is giving that feels chosen even when it is difficult.

When sacrifice becomes chronic and unreciprocated, something shifts internally. You may still care, but caring no longer feels alive. It feels obligatory, heavy, or overdone.

In these moments, people often tell themselves they are being noble.

"I'm just putting them first."

"This is what love requires."

"They need me more than I need myself right now."

But love does not require the permanent postponement of your own life.

And when a relationship demands that you consistently silence your needs, suppress your resentment, and override your intuition, it is no longer asking for love. It is asking for compliance.

This distinction matters because many readers assume that if they step back, they will lose the capacity to love at all.

In reality, the opposite is often true.

When obligation loosens, something unexpected can happen. Love becomes quieter, but clearer. Less frantic, more grounded. Less performative, more honest.

For some people, stepping back reveals that love is still there, but it needs new structure. For others, it reveals that what they were calling love was actually fear, guilt, or habit.

Both discoveries are painful. Both are clarifying.

Love without self-erasure leaves room for dignity.

It does not require you to shrink.

It does not require you to disappear.

It does not require you to betray yourself to preserve connection.

This is also where conditional love often gets misunderstood.

Many readers bristle at the idea that love should be conditional, but conditional does not mean fragile or withholding.

It means bounded.

It means love exists within reality, not fantasy.

It means care is offered without surrendering agency.

It means connection is sustained by choice, not fear.

Unconditional love, when applied to adult relationships, often becomes a justification for limitless tolerance. It asks people to stay no matter the cost, no matter the imbalance, no matter the erosion.

That is not intimacy. That is captivity.

Love that respects both people requires conditions. Not as threats, but as truths.

Conditions like:

- Mutual responsibility
- Emotional safety
- Respect for boundaries
- Space for growth on both sides

When those conditions disappear, love does not automatically disappear. But it does change.

And sometimes, the most loving thing you can do is stop participating in a dynamic that requires you to vanish.

This chapter is not asking you to decide whether to stay or leave.

It is asking you to examine whether your version of love still includes you.

In the next section, we will turn toward guilt more directly. We will look at the different forms it takes, why it feels so convincing, and how to move through it without becoming cold, defensive, or morally untethered.

Section 5: Guilt, Moral Injury, and the Cost of Staying

By the time readers reach this part of the chapter, many of them are not confused about their exhaustion.

They are confused about their guilt.

They know something feels wrong in the relationship. They know they are depleted. They may even know, intellectually, that continuing as they are is unsustainable.

And yet, guilt remains the loudest voice in the room.

This guilt is not simple. It is layered, persuasive, and deeply tied to identity.

In my clinical experience, people often assume guilt is a signal that they are doing something wrong. But in obligation-based relationships, guilt is often a signal that you are doing something *different* from what you were trained to do.

To understand this, it helps to slow down and name the types of guilt that tend to surface here.

The Many Faces of Guilt

Not all guilt comes from the same place, even though it often feels the same in the body. Many readers assume guilt means they are doing something wrong, when in fact it often reflects an identity shift."

Type	Source	Focus
Moral	Your actions	Right vs. Wrong
Emotional	Other people's feelings	Connection vs. Disappointment
Identity	Your self-image	Ideal Self vs. Real Self
Survivor	Your fortune/luck	Fairness vs. Randomness

Moral guilt is about right versus wrong.
It asks, "Am I violating my values?"

Emotional guilt is about other people's feelings.
It asks, "Am I hurting someone I care about?"

Identity guilt is about self-image.
It asks, "Who am I if I don't do this anymore?"

Survivor guilt is about fairness.
It asks, "Why do I get relief while they struggle?"

At this stage of the book, many readers experience all four. But identity guilt is often the most destabilizing.

When love has been equated with endurance, stepping back does not just feel uncomfortable. It feels like a threat to who you are.

People say things like:

- "I'm not the kind of person who leaves."
- "I've always been the reliable one."

- "If I stop helping, what does that make me?"
- "I don't recognize myself when I say no."

It is okay to grieve an identity that was built around being needed.

Identity guilt lingers longer than other forms of guilt because it cannot be resolved by logic alone. You cannot reason your way out of it by listing pros and cons. It softens only as a new identity begins to take shape.

That takes time.

Moral Injury: When Values Are Used Against You

Moral injury occurs when a person's values are repeatedly used to justify harm to themselves. Not harm inflicted by others directly, but harm created through internal coercion.

For example:

- Staying because "good people don't abandon others"
- Enduring because "love means sacrifice"
- Continuing because "they can't handle it without me"

Over time, these values stop functioning as guides and start functioning as restraints.

In my clinical experience, this is where people become emotionally numb, irritable, or quietly resentful. They are not heartless. They are injured.

They are being asked to violate their own limits in the name of morality.

This is why obligation feels so heavy in the body. It is not just fatigue. It is moral dissonance.

You are doing something that conflicts with your internal truth, and your nervous system knows it.

The Cost of Staying in Obligation

Many readers ask, often quietly, "But what's the harm if I just keep going?"

The harm is rarely immediate. It accumulates slowly.

Over time, staying in obligation tends to erode:

- Mental health, through chronic anxiety, resentment, and burnout
- Intimacy, as closeness becomes associated with pressure rather than warmth
- Parenting capacity, as emotional bandwidth is drained elsewhere
- Self-respect, as your needs become negotiable, but everyone else's are not
- The relationship itself, as care turns into quiet bitterness

One of the most painful ironies is that obligation often reduces the very love it is trying to preserve.

People become less patient. Less generous. Less emotionally available to those they genuinely want to show up for, including children, partners, and themselves.

They may still be physically present, but internally they are gone.

That is not a moral failure. It is a predictable outcome of prolonged over-functioning.

What Guilt Is Not Telling You

Guilt often tells a very convincing story:

"If you step back, you are abandoning."

"If you choose yourself, you are selfish."

"If you stop, you are cruel."

But guilt does not ask whether the relationship is mutual.

It does not ask whether the dynamic is sustainable.

It does not ask whether love still feels alive.

It simply asks whether you are willing to keep paying the cost.

Guilt does not disappear immediately when you step back. Often, it intensifies before it softens. This is especially true for people whose identity has long been tied to being needed.

The presence of guilt does not mean you are doing something wrong. Often, it means you are doing something new.

Holding Guilt Without Letting It Decide

Guilt cannot be the authority in your life.

You can acknowledge guilt without obeying it.

You can feel guilt without using it as a compass.

You can care deeply without surrendering your integrity.

For some people, guilt gradually transforms into grief.

For others, it transforms into clarity.

For many, it does both.

In the next section, we will introduce a simple internal test that helps distinguish love from obligation in real time. It should help you listen more accurately to what your body and mind are already telling you.

Section 6: A Quiet Test for Love Versus Obligation

By now, many readers are no longer asking, *"Is this relationship hard?"*

They are asking something more precise and more unsettling:

"Why does it feel so heavy to stay?"

This is where love and obligation finally need to be separated.

Not to force a decision.

Not to justify leaving.

But to tell the truth about what is actually driving your behavior.

Why an Internal Test Matters

Obligation is persuasive because it sounds reasonable.

It borrows the language of virtue.

It recruits loyalty, responsibility, and compassion.

It disguises itself as character.

That is why people stay stuck for so long. They are not confused about their suffering. They are confused about what it *means*.

An internal test helps cut through rationalization without turning you into a villain in your own story.

It does not ask what you *should* do.

It asks what your nervous system already knows.

The Love vs. Obligation Check-In

These questions are not meant to be answered quickly. They are meant to be noticed.

You may not like your answers at first. That does not make them wrong.

Ask yourself:

When I imagine continuing exactly as things are for another year, do I feel steadier or smaller?

When I imagine stepping back, do I feel grief, relief, or both?

Before interacting with this person, does my body soften or brace?

When I give, do I feel expanded afterward or quietly depleted?

If no one judged me, praised me, or condemned me, would I still choose this?

If someone else were asking the same thing of me, would I say yes just as easily?

Do I enjoy giving here, or do I endure it?

Love can include grief.

Love can include sadness.

Love can include sacrifice.

But love does not require constant self-erasure to survive.

Signals Obligation Is Driving the Relationship

In my clinical experience, obligation leaves a very specific footprint.

Readers often describe:

- Dreading seeing the person's name on their phone
- Taking a deep breath before responding, as if preparing for impact
- Feeling anxious or irritable during contact
- Needing to rehearse responses to avoid conflict
- Rationalizing exhaustion instead of questioning it
- Staying because leaving feels morally impossible, not emotionally unwanted

None of these make you cold or unloving. Your system is simply under strain.

Obligation keeps relationships alive by pressure.

Love keeps them alive by choice.

What This Chapter Is *Not* Saying

It is important to be very clear about this.

This chapter is not anti-commitment.

It is not pro-abandonment.

It is not an endorsement of impulsive exits.

It is not saying, "You don't owe anyone anything."

And it is certainly not encouraging anger, contempt, or emotional withdrawal.

This is not about burning bridges.

It is about noticing which ones are being held up by you alone.

You can care without collapsing.

You can love without disappearing.

You can step back without becoming cruel.

Love With Limits Is Still Love

One of the most destabilizing beliefs readers carry is that love must be unconditional to be real.

In my clinical experience, unconditional love is often confused with unconditional tolerance.

Real love has conditions.

Not transactional conditions, but relational ones.

Conditions like:

- Mutual respect
- Emotional reciprocity
- Shared responsibility
- The ability to say no without fear

When those conditions disappear, love does not deepen. It deforms.

You are not failing love by noticing this.

You are honoring it.

A Quiet Place to Land

If you are unsure what comes next, that is okay.

This chapter is not asking you to decide today.

It is asking you to stop lying to yourself about why you stay.

You may choose to remain.

You may choose to detach.

You may choose to renegotiate.

You may choose to leave later, or not at all.

What matters is that your choice comes from clarity, not coercion.

From desire, not duty.

From care, not captivity.

If you remember nothing else from this chapter, let it be this:

Love feels chosen.

Obligation feels compulsory.

And you are allowed to tell the difference.

That permission alone changes everything.

Section 7: Choosing Love Without Losing Yourself

By the time people reach the end of this chapter, they are often expecting a directive.

Something like:

Now leave.

Now stay.

Now set this boundary.

Now decide.

But no one can make these decisions for you.

This book cannot tell you what to do, or what's right for you. Instead, it will hopefully teach you to better listen to yourself and your own needs.

Why This Distinction Matters More Than the Decision

Many readers believe the most important question is whether they stay or go.

In my clinical experience, the more important question is *why*.

Two people can make the same external choice for entirely different internal reasons, and have completely different outcomes.

You can stay out of love and remain whole.

You can stay out of obligation and slowly disappear.

You can leave with care and integrity.

You can leave in panic and self-reproach.

The outcome is shaped less by the decision itself and more by the internal posture behind it.

This chapter is about correcting that posture.

Releasing the Moral Narrative

One of the quietest but most damaging forces in obligation-based relationships is the moral story people tell themselves.

"I'm the good one."

"I'm the strong one."

"I'm the one who doesn't give up."

"I'm not like people who leave."

These identities feel stabilizing at first. They give meaning to suffering.

But over time, they become cages.

When your worth depends on endurance, clarity feels like betrayal.

When your goodness depends on self-sacrifice, relief feels immoral.

When your identity depends on being needed, independence feels threatening.

Letting go of obligation often means letting go of a version of yourself that once felt virtuous.

What Love Looks Like After Obligation Loosens

When obligation loosens, love often changes shape.

It may become quieter.

Less dramatic.

Less fused.

Less urgent.

For some people, love becomes lighter.

For others, it becomes more distant.

For some, it becomes clearer that what they were calling love was actually fear, guilt, or responsibility holding everything together.

None of these outcomes mean you failed.

They mean the relationship is no longer being artificially sustained.

Love that survives clarity is real love.

Love that collapses when obligation is removed was never sustainable to begin with.

You Are Not Cruel for Wanting Room to Breathe

Many readers are waiting for permission to want space without hatred.

To want relief without abandonment.

To want themselves back without destroying someone else.

Here it is.

You are allowed to want a relationship that does not require self-erasure.

You are allowed to notice when giving feels draining instead of nourishing.

You are allowed to choose sustainability over martyrdom.

You are allowed to stop performing goodness at your own expense.

A Final Reframe to Carry Forward

If you find yourself wondering whether you are loving enough, ask a different question:

Am I choosing this freely, or am I complying out of fear?

Love can coexist with grief.

Love can coexist with limits.

Love can coexist with distance.

What love cannot coexist with, indefinitely, is captivity.

You do not have to punish yourself to prove you care.

You do not have to suffer to justify connection.

You do not have to disappear to keep someone else comfortable.

Love is not measured by how much you endure.

It is measured by how much of yourself remains intact.

If this chapter gave you language for something you already felt but could not name, that is enough for now.

Clarity comes before change.
Truth comes before action.
Permission comes before peace.
And you are allowed to take those steps in that order.
Quietly.
Deliberately.
Without apology.

CHAPTER 11

When to Seek Help

Section 1: Needing Help Is Not a Failure of Boundaries

By the time people reach this chapter, many of them are already doing a great deal of work.

They have read. They have reflected. They have set limits. They have pulled back from rescuing, stopped over-functioning, and tried to hold boundaries with more clarity than ever before.

And yet, something still feels stuck.

When this happens, people often reach a painful conclusion: *If I still need help, I must be doing something wrong.*

They assume that needing support means their boundaries failed, their insight wasn't deep enough, or their resolve wasn't strong enough. None of this negative self-talk is true.

Needing help is not a failure of boundaries. It is often evidence that you have reached the natural limits of what self-work can do on its own.

Boundaries are a powerful tool. Insight is essential. Awareness matters. But there are dynamics that cannot be fully resolved in isolation, especially when long-standing emotional patterns, chronic stress, or entrenched roles are involved.

Knowing when to seek help requires strength, not weakness. It requires awareness, humility, and honesty about what you can and cannot carry alone.

Many readers hesitate here because they believe that seeking help means they are "backtracking." They worry that asking for support somehow undoes the progress they've made. In reality, the opposite is usually true. Seeking help is often the next responsible step *because* you have already done so much.

Seeking help is not giving up. You are simply recognizing that the work you have done may need some reinforcement. Reaching for structure is wise.

Support will only reinforce your boundaries.

One of the most damaging myths in self-growth culture is the idea that strength means doing everything on your own. This belief quietly turns independence into isolation and resilience into endurance. Over time, it leaves people exhausted, emotionally numb, or quietly shut down.

When you have tried to set limits, regulate your reactions, communicate clearly, and still feel depleted or stuck, it does not mean you need to try harder. It may mean that the work now requires another layer of support.

Importantly, you do not have to wait for a crisis to justify help.

You do not need to be falling apart. You do not need to be in danger. You do not need to reach a breaking point to deserve support. Waiting until things become unmanageable often increases the cost of recovery, not the clarity.

Seeking help early is often an act of responsibility, not desperation.

Some readers worry that reaching out for help means something is "wrong" with them. Others fear it means they are betraying the person they care about, or admitting defeat in the relationship. These fears are understandable, especially for people who have spent years being the stable one, the reliable one, the one who holds things together.

But seeking help does not mean you are abandoning the relationship. It does not mean you are giving up. And it does not mean you have failed.

It means you are taking your own well-being seriously.

It might be time to reach for help. Sometimes self-work alone is not enough, and you can approach support without shame, panic, or moral judgment.

You are not weak for needing help.

You are responding to reality.

And responding to reality, rather than forcing yourself to endure it silently, is one of the most mature decisions a person can make.

Section 2: When Self-Work Stops Being Enough

There is a point at which effort alone stops producing movement.

Many readers reach this stage quietly. They are not in crisis. They are not dramatic. They are not unraveling in obvious ways. Instead, they feel worn down, flattened, or emotionally shut off. The urgency that once drove them to set boundaries has faded, not because things improved, but because they are tired of trying.

This is one of the clearest signals that self-work has reached its limit.

Self-help tools work best when there is enough emotional bandwidth to use them. When that bandwidth is depleted, even the best insight can start to feel hollow. People know what they *should* do, but no longer feel the energy or conviction to do it.

This often shows up as emotional numbness.

Readers describe feeling indifferent where they once felt anxious. They stop reacting, not because they are regulated, but because they are burned out. They may give in more easily, avoid difficult conversations, or disengage altogether. On the surface, it can look like acceptance. Internally, it feels like checking out.

Loss of functioning is another important marker.

You may notice that tasks you once handled easily now feel heavy. Concentration suffers. Motivation drops. Sleep becomes irregular. Small decisions feel overwhelming. Some readers stop caring about consequences that would have mattered deeply to them before. This is not laziness or avoidance. It is often the nervous system conserving energy after prolonged strain.

Another common sign is repeated cycling despite insight.

You understand the dynamic. You can name the pattern. You may even predict how interactions will unfold. And yet, the cycle keeps repeating. Boundaries are set, then eroded. Distance is created, then closed. Each round feels more exhausting than the last.

When insight no longer leads to change, more insight is rarely the answer.

Some readers experience escalating anxiety or depression during this phase. Others feel the opposite. They become emotionally flat, detached, or apathetic. Both responses signal that the system is under strain. Chronic stress does not always look like panic. Sometimes it looks like numbness.

Obsessive rumination can also appear here.

You replay conversations. You analyze decisions. You think through scenarios repeatedly without resolution. This mental looping often reflects a stalled system, not a lack of effort. The mind is trying to solve a problem that cannot be solved internally alone.

It is also common to see deterioration in other relationships.

When emotional energy is consumed by one unresolved dynamic, there is less available for the rest of life. Readers may notice increased irritability with children, withdrawal from friends, or emotional distance from partners who are not part of the dependent relationship. This is often accompanied by guilt and confusion.

At this stage, many people tell themselves they simply need to try harder.

They minimize their distress by comparing it to others. They say things like, "Other people have it worse," or "I shouldn't need help for something like this." They assume that seeking support means admitting failure.

These beliefs delay relief rather than preserve strength.

When you are burned out, trying harder does not restore capacity.

Struggle does not automatically mean you need help. Growth is uncomfortable, and discomfort alone is not a reason to escalate care. But when effort leads to shutdown rather than adaptation, when boundaries no longer stabilize you, and when insight no longer translates into action, it is often time to add support.

Self-work is meant to expand capacity, not replace care. When the work starts to feel like endurance rather than development, something needs reinforcement.

Seeking help at this point is not giving up.

It is recognizing that the work now requires more than one set of hands.

In the next section, we will look at the different types of help available, and how to think about them without confusion, stigma, or the fear of "doing it wrong."

Section 3: What Kind of Help Fits the Problem

One of the reasons people delay seeking help is not resistance. It is confusion.

They know something is no longer working, but they do not know what kind of support would actually help. Therapy feels vague. Medication feels loaded. Support groups feel unfamiliar. And many people worry that choosing the "wrong" kind of help will make things worse rather than better.

So let's simplify this.

Seeking help does not mean committing to a single path forever. It means choosing a form of support that matches the problem you are dealing with *right now*.

Different kinds of help do different things.

Individual Therapy: When You Need Clarity, Containment, and Agency

Individual therapy is often the most appropriate starting point for readers at this stage.

It is especially helpful when:

- You feel emotionally depleted, numb, or shut down
- You are stuck in rumination or self-doubt
- You need help sorting out guilt, fear, and responsibility
- You want support that centers *your* experience rather than the relationship as a whole

Good individual therapy is not about telling you what to do. It is about helping you hear yourself more clearly without distortion. It should strengthen your sense of agency, not replace it.

In my clinical experience, the most effective therapy at this stage does three things:

- It validates reality without minimizing it
- It helps regulate the nervous system, so thinking becomes clearer
- It supports action without moralizing it

If therapy leaves you feeling smaller, more confused, or increasingly dependent on the therapist's opinion, something is off. Therapy should help you tolerate ambiguity, not erase it by outsourcing decisions.

Psychiatry and Medication: When Symptoms Are Blocking Function

Medication is not a solution to unhealthy dynamics. It is not meant to make intolerable situations tolerable forever.

But medication *can* be appropriate when symptoms are interfering with your ability to think, function, or act.

I most often recommend considering medication when:

- Anxiety or panic is debilitating
- Depression is flattening motivation or energy
- Sleep, concentration, or appetite are significantly impaired
- Emotional distress is leading to substance use or avoidance

Medication can reduce suffering enough to create space. Space to think. Space to feel. Space to make decisions that are not driven purely by overwhelm.

The goal is not numbness. The goal is clarity.

There is an important boundary here.

Medication should not be used to tolerate abuse, coercion, or chronic harm. If the primary function of medication becomes "so I can endure this," something needs to be reassessed. Used thoughtfully, medication supports agency. Used defensively, it can delay change.

Support Groups: When Validation and Shared Reality Matter

Support groups can be powerful when they are specific and well-matched to your needs.

Hearing others describe experiences that mirror your own can dissolve isolation quickly. It helps normalize reactions that people often shame themselves for having. It also provides perspective that is hard to access alone.

Support groups are especially useful when:

- You feel alone or misunderstood
- Shame is keeping you silent
- You need confirmation that you are not "imagining" the problem

They are not a substitute for therapy, but they can complement it well. I find they are often particularly useful for people in dependent dynamics.

The key is specificity. Groups that are too broad often miss the nuance of dependent dynamics. Groups that are focused on shared patterns tend to be more grounding and less overwhelming. Find a group for people going through similar struggles, such as Codependents Anonymous.

Couples or Family Therapy: When Both People Are Willing Participants

Couples or family therapy can be helpful, but only under certain conditions.

It works best when:

- Both people want to be there
- Both are willing to examine their own behavior
- The therapist does not function as a referee or moral judge

Joint therapy is not helpful when one person attends reluctantly, defensively, or with the expectation that the therapist will "fix" the other person. It can also be harmful if it pressures someone to compromise boundaries for the sake of harmony.

In dependent dynamics, joint therapy too early can reinforce imbalance. If one person is doing most of the emotional work, therapy can become another place where responsibility is unevenly distributed.

Sometimes individual stabilization needs to come first.

Coaching: When Structure and Accountability Are the Primary Needs

Coaching can be useful for readers who are emotionally regulated but stuck in action.

If insight is present and emotions are manageable, but follow-through is inconsistent, coaching can provide structure without delving deeply into emotional processing.

Coaching is not therapy. It should not be used to treat depression, anxiety disorders, or trauma. But it can support execution when capacity is already in place.

Choosing Without Overthinking

Many readers want certainty before choosing help. They want to know the *perfect* option, but perfection doesn't exist.

In most cases, the best choice is the one that reduces suffering enough to restore movement. You can adjust later. You can switch providers. You can add or remove layers of support. You can always adjust the amount and type of help you're seeking to best suit your needs.

In the next section, we will talk about red flags and safety concerns, and how to name them clearly without catastrophizing or panic.

Section 4: Red Flags That Mean You Should Not Handle This Alone

Most people typically miss red flags because they minimize, normalize, or rationalize them. Some awareness is there.

People in dependent relationships have often learned to tolerate a great deal. They have adjusted their expectations downward. They have reframed behavior. They have told themselves, "This is just how things are right now," or "I can handle it."

This section is not meant to scare you. It is meant to clarify when self-work, boundaries, and insight are no longer enough on their own.

There are situations where outside help is not optional. It is responsible.

The Difference Between Difficulty and Danger

Not all distress is dangerous.

Feeling sad, guilty, anxious, or uncertain after setting boundaries is part of growth. Emotional discomfort alone does not mean you need urgent intervention.

What matters is **trajectory and intensity**, not isolated moments.

The line is crossed when symptoms begin to:

- Impair basic functioning
- Escalate rather than stabilize
- Push you toward behaviors that compromise safety, judgment, or health

When coping shifts into collapse, it is time to widen the circle of support.

Psychological Red Flags That Require Help

Some experiences should never be managed in isolation.

These include:

- Thoughts of hurting yourself or others
- Persistent fantasies of revenge, harm, or retaliation
- Hearing voices or seeing things that others do not
- Severe panic attacks that feel uncontrollable or disabling
- Prolonged emotional numbness or detachment
- Significant changes in sleep, appetite, concentration, or energy
- Losing interest in things that once mattered to you

These are not moral failures. They are signals.

They indicate that your nervous system is overwhelmed and that willpower alone is no longer sufficient.

Substance Use as a Warning Sign

One of the most common red flags I see clinically is the quiet increase in substance use.

It may look like:

- Drinking to fall asleep
- Using substances to tolerate contact or conversations
- Needing something to "take the edge off" regularly
- Using substances to avoid thinking or feeling

When substances become a primary coping tool, they often mask distress while amplifying long-term harm.

If substances are being used to manage emotional pain related to a relationship or dynamic, outside help is important. Not because you are weak, but because the risk of escalation is real.

When Boundaries Increase Risk Instead of Safety

Boundaries are meant to increase stability. When they instead lead to escalating danger, support is essential.

This includes situations where:

- Boundaries trigger threats of self-harm
- You are told you will be responsible for catastrophic outcomes
- Emotional pressure escalates into intimidation
- You feel afraid to hold limits

You are not required to manage another person's mental health alone.

If holding boundaries makes you fear for safety, that is a sign the situation exceeds what self-help can address.

Isolation as a Critical Signal

Isolation often sneaks in quietly.

You may stop sharing what is happening because:

- You do not want to worry others
- You are tired of explaining
- You fear judgment
- You feel ashamed for "still being here"

Isolation increases risk because it removes perspective.

In my clinical work, isolation is one of the strongest predictors that someone will wait too long to seek help. Not because they do not know better, but because they feel alone with it.

If you find yourself withdrawing from friends, family, or activities you once enjoyed, that is not something to push through alone.

Talking About Crisis Without Panic

Naming red flags does not mean assuming the worst.

It means being honest about capacity.

If you are experiencing any of the signs above, seeking help does not mean something terrible is about to happen. It means you are taking responsibility before things deteriorate further.

Support at this stage is preventive, not reactive.

You do not need to wait for collapse to justify care.

A Grounding Reminder

Needing help does not invalidate the work you have already done.

It does not mean your boundaries failed.

It does not mean you misjudged the situation.

It does not mean you are incapable.

It means you are responding to reality as it is now, not as you wish it to be.

In the next section, we will talk about shame, guilt, and moral judgment around seeking help, and how to release the belief that needing support makes you weak, dramatic, or disloyal.

Section 5: Releasing Shame Around Seeking Help

For many readers, the greatest barrier to seeking help is not access, money, or time.

It is shame.

By the time people consider professional support, they have often already endured more than they should have. They have tried self-reflection, communication, boundaries, restraint, patience, and sacrifice. When those efforts do not resolve the situation, they do not immediately think, *I need support.*

They think, *I must be failing.*

The Quiet Shame People Carry

In my clinical experience, shame around seeking help usually takes one of a few forms:

- Feeling weak or inadequate
- Believing you should be able to handle this alone
- Feeling disloyal to the dependent person
- Worrying that asking for help means you are "giving up"
- Fearing judgment from family, culture, or community

For many men, shame sounds like:

"I should be able to fix this."

"I'm not strong enough if I need help."

"I'm supposed to handle my own problems."

For many women, shame sounds like:

"I'm being too emotional."

"I'm overreacting."

"I should be more patient or understanding."

These beliefs are not truths. They are cultural scripts.

They keep people suffering quietly long after support would have helped.

Help-Seeking Is Not Disloyalty

One of the most painful myths readers carry is the idea that seeking help betrays the dependent person or the relationship.

This is especially true in family-centered or collectivist cultures, where loyalty and endurance are moral virtues. In those contexts, needing help can feel like exposing the family, airing private struggles, or failing to protect someone you love.

But seeking help does not mean you are giving up on the relationship. In many cases, it means you are trying to save what can be saved.

It means you are acknowledging that the current dynamic is unsustainable and that continuing alone will only deepen resentment, numbness, or collapse.

Strength, Not Failure

There is a western cultural fantasy that strong people solve things internally.

In reality, strong people recognize when a system requires reinforcement.

In medicine, no one expects a broken bone to heal without support.

In business, no leader is expected to manage growth alone.

In athletics, training without a coach is rarely effective.

Yet in emotional life, we expect people to endure indefinitely without assistance.

That expectation is unrealistic and damaging.

Seeking help is not evidence that boundaries failed. It is evidence that you noticed your limits before harm occurred.

When Shame Masquerades as Morality

Shame often disguises itself as moral reasoning.

It sounds like:

"I should be able to tolerate this."

"I owe them this."

"I don't have the right to need more."

You are allowed to seek support without first proving that things are "bad enough."

Pain does not require comparison to be valid. Suffering does not need to reach catastrophe to deserve care.

Seeking Help Does Not Hand Over Control

Another common fear is that seeking help means surrendering agency.

Readers worry:

"What if a therapist tells me to leave?"

"What if medication changes who I am?"

"What if getting help means someone else decides for me?"

This fear keeps people stuck.

Support does not replace your judgment. It strengthens it.

Good help does not dictate outcomes. It expands your capacity to think clearly, tolerate emotion, and make choices aligned with your values rather than your fear.

You are not outsourcing your life.

You are resourcing it.

The Cost of Waiting Too Long

In my clinical experience, the people who suffer most are often the ones who waited the longest.

Not because they were weak, but because they were afraid of what seeking help would say about them.

Delay often leads to:

- Emotional numbness
- Increased resentment
- Escalation into anxiety or depression
- Greater damage to the relationship
- Fewer options when help finally arrives

Seeking help earlier preserves flexibility. Waiting out of shame often narrows it.

A Reframe Worth Holding

Try holding this frame instead:

Needing help does not invalidate your progress.

It does not erase the work you have done.

It does not mean you failed to love well.

It means you respected reality enough to stop pretending you could do this alone.

That is not weakness.

That is maturity.

In the final section, we will talk about how to choose the *right* kind of help, what to listen for in providers, and how to avoid support that unintentionally reinforces guilt, dependence, or stagnation.

Section 6: Seeking Help Is Not Surrender

By the time someone reaches this point, something important has already happened.

They have tried.

They have reflected.

They have set boundaries.

They have communicated clearly.They have tolerated discomfort.

They have carried responsibility longer than most people ever see.

Seeking help at this stage is not a collapse of effort. It is the natural next step when effort alone is no longer enough.

One of the most damaging myths around mental health support is the idea that help is something you turn to only after you've failed. That therapy, medication, or outside support are last resorts for people who could not handle things on their own.

In my clinical experience, the opposite is far more often true.

The people who seek help appropriately are usually the ones who have been holding too much for too long.

They are not weak.

They are depleted.

They are not avoiding responsibility.

They are finally recognizing the limits of what one person can sustainably carry.

There is an important distinction here.

Needing help does not invalidate the progress you have made.

It does not erase the insight you have gained.

It does not mean your boundaries were ineffective.

And it does not mean you gave up on the relationship.

It means you have reached the edge of what self-work can accomplish in isolation.

Some dynamics cannot be untangled alone, especially when:

- The nervous system is chronically activated
- Emotional numbness has replaced feeling
- Functioning has begun to decline
- Rumination has overtaken clarity
- Or the cost of continuing without support is becoming harder to ignore

At this point, seeking help is not a retreat.

It is an act of responsibility.

For many readers, the most painful barrier to seeking help is shame.

Men often frame it as failure or weakness, a fear of not being "strong enough."

Women often frame it as being dramatic, needy, or overly emotional.

Across cultures, there can be fears of disloyalty, exposure, or betrayal of family values.

These narratives keep people suffering quietly far longer than they need to.

Seeking help does not mean you are abandoning anyone.

It does not mean you are turning your back on love, commitment, or care.

It does not mean you are asking someone else to solve your life.

It means you are choosing support over isolation.

It means you are giving yourself the same seriousness and care you have likely given everyone else.

There is also no requirement that things be "bad enough" to justify help.

You do not need to wait for collapse.

You do not need to reach crisis.

You do not need to compare your pain to someone else's trauma.

If you are exhausted, numb, stuck, or quietly unraveling, that is enough information.

In my clinical work, the people who suffer most are often the ones who waited the longest.

Not because they were careless, but because they believed they had to endure more to earn support.

Endurance is not a virtue when it comes at the cost of your mental health.

Help is not something that takes your agency away.

When done well, it gives it back to you.

A good therapist does not decide for you.

A thoughtful clinician does not push you toward outcomes you are not ready for.

Appropriate support helps you think more clearly, regulate more effectively, and act from choice rather than fear.

It creates space.

It reduces suffering.

It restores perspective.

And most importantly, it reminds you that you do not have to do this alone.

A Grounding Checklist

You may want to consider seeking help if several of the following are true:

- You feel emotionally numb, burned out, or detached from yourself
- You are repeating the same cycles despite insight and effort
- Your anxiety, depression, or panic is worsening or interfering with daily life
- You are losing functioning, motivation, or hope
- You are using substances, avoidance, or withdrawal to cope

- You feel stuck between guilt and exhaustion with no relief in sight
- You have set boundaries, but feel overwhelmed holding them alone

If you see yourself here, this is not a judgment.

You have not failed, but you may have reached a point where support is appropriate, and asking for help takes strength.

You are allowed to protect your mental health.

You are allowed to ask for support.

You are allowed to stop doing this alone.

That choice does not undo your progress.

It honors it.

CHAPTER 12

Deciding to Stay or Go

Section 1: The Question Everyone Tries to Outsource

There is a moment almost everyone reaches, usually quietly, when the question stops being theoretical.

Should I stay, or should I go?

People rarely arrive at this question casually. By the time it shows up, most have already tried explaining, accommodating, waiting, adjusting, forgiving, and hoping. They have read articles. They have talked to friends. They may have been in therapy. They may have told themselves, many times, that things will settle if they are just more patient or more understanding.

What makes this question so heavy is not that it is complicated. It is that people desperately want someone else to answer it for them.

They ask therapists. They ask friends. They ask family members. They ask books like this one. They hope that somewhere, someone with enough authority will tell them what to do so they do not have to carry the responsibility of the decision themselves.

I want to be clear from the start. I cannot tell you whether you should stay or go. And more importantly, I should not.

Not because I am avoiding responsibility, but because this is not a decision that can be made from the outside. The moment someone else decides for you, the outcome will never fully belong to you. And when the grief, doubt, or second-guessing arrives, it always does, you will feel even more unmoored.

Most people already know when it is time to leave.

That knowing is not dramatic. It is not always loud. It does not arrive with certainty or anger. Often, it shows up as a quiet sense of relief when you imagine being free of the constant effort. A feeling of lightness when you picture your days no longer organized around managing someone else's emotions. A subtle but persistent sense that staying is costing you more than you can afford.

At the same time, knowing is often buried under guilt.

People confuse guilt with love. They confuse responsibility with care. They tell themselves that wanting out must mean they are selfish, ungrateful, or weak. They look for permission to leave so they do not have to trust their own judgment.

Others experience the opposite confusion. They feel connected. They feel hopeful. They still see movement, effort, or change. And they worry that leaving too soon would be an act of avoidance rather than wisdom.

If you are still deeply connected, still able to imagine a future that feels alive rather than burdensome, there is no prize for leaving early. Walking away should not be a flex. It should not be used to prove strength, independence, or emotional sophistication. Leaving is not inherently more evolved than staying.

But if you find that you have exhausted your options, that the effort required to remain is slowly hollowing you out, and that the idea of leaving feels less like abandonment and more like oxygen, that knowing matters.

Most people are not confused because they lack information. They are confused because the emotional noise is loud.

Guilt. Fear. Responsibility. Hope. Loyalty.

When those voices quiet, even briefly, the answer often becomes clearer than people expect.

Section 2: Why People Leave Too Early and Why That Matters

In recent years, the cultural message around relationships has shifted in an important but imperfect way. Many people have been taught, correctly, that suffering is not a requirement for love. That boundaries matter. That staying in relationships that harm you is not noble.

But alongside that necessary correction, another distortion has emerged.

Discomfort is increasingly treated as evidence that something is wrong.

Effort is framed as settling. Frustration is pathologized. Emotional labor is seen as something to be avoided at all costs. At the first sign of turbulence, many people are encouraged to interpret their distress as proof that the relationship itself is unhealthy.

This is not always true.

All meaningful relationships require work. They require patience, repair, tolerance for frustration, and the ability to stay present when things are not smooth. Growth rarely feels good while it is happening. If the standard for staying is that things must feel easy, calm, and affirming at all times, very few relationships will survive.

All relationships require tolerating some about of distress and discomfort.

From a low tolerance for emotional discomfort. From fear of conflict. From the belief that if something is hard, it must be wrong. From the hope that relief itself is the same thing as wisdom.

Relief is seductive. When you step away from a difficult dynamic, anxiety drops quickly. The nervous system settles. The quiet feels intoxicating. That does not automatically mean the decision was wrong. But it also does not automatically mean it was right.

Some people mistake the absence of discomfort for healing. Others mistake the return of discomfort for danger.

Leaving prematurely often leaves unfinished emotional business behind. Patterns repeat. New relationships recreate the same dynamics under different names. The work that was avoided does not disappear. It simply waits.

This book does not glorify endurance for endurance's sake. It does not suggest that you should stay in relationships that are eroding your sense of self. But it does respect honest effort.

Trying matters.

There is a difference between staying because you are afraid to leave and staying because you believe, based on evidence, that growth is possible. There is also a difference between leaving because you are being harmed and leaving because you cannot tolerate the vulnerability that real relationship work requires.

Modern language sometimes collapses these distinctions. It uses the same vocabulary for abuse and for inconvenience, for harm and for frustration. When everything is framed as a threat to mental health, it becomes harder to tell when a relationship truly needs to end and when it is simply asking something of you.

Leaving without trying does not make someone empowered. It often makes them avoidant.

Trying does not guarantee success. Staying is not always the mature choice. It means that effort clarifies things. It teaches you what is possible and what is not. It allows you to leave, if you do leave, with far less doubt and far less regret.

Many people who struggle the most after leaving are not those who stayed too long. They are those who left without fully understanding what they were leaving, or why.

Section 3: When Staying Is a Real Choice (Not a Fantasy)

Staying is often talked about as if it is the passive option. As if remaining means doing nothing, while leaving represents action, courage, or self-respect. In reality, staying in a difficult relationship can be one of the most active and demanding choices a person makes.

But staying is only a real choice when it is grounded in evidence.

Hope alone is not enough. Insight alone is not enough. Love alone is not enough. Movement and change are necessary.

In relationships shaped by dependency, many people confuse awareness with change. A partner may be able to describe their anxiety in detail, understand their patterns intellectually, or even apologize sincerely after things escalate. While insight can be meaningful, it does not, by itself, alter the structure of the relationship. Understanding a problem does not automatically change how someone behaves when they are overwhelmed.

Staying becomes viable when insight translates into behavior.

The clearest indicator is not what someone says in moments of calm, but what happens when stress returns. Are boundaries respected more often than they are violated? Does distress lead to self-regulation more than collapse? Are you being asked to rescue less, even if imperfectly? These are the quiet signs that something is shifting.

Behavioral change rarely looks dramatic. It is often subtle and uneven. Progress may be slow. There may still be setbacks. What matters is direction.

When someone is genuinely working on dependency, you begin to notice that the intensity decreases over time. The urgency softens. The crises become less frequent. They may still struggle, but they tolerate that struggle with less panic and less pressure on you to fix it.

Another underappreciated marker of real change is being given space without punishment.

If hours pass and you are not flooded with messages, accusations, or emotional fallout, that matters. Quiet that feels peaceful rather than anxious is not empty. It is capacity. It suggests that the nervous system is learning to settle without constant external regulation.

This is often missed because it does not announce itself. There is no grand declaration of independence. There is just more room to breathe.

Staying also requires your own capacity.

Even when change is happening, staying demands patience and tolerance for frustration. Growth is rarely linear. There will be moments where old patterns reappear, especially under stress. Staying is not about ignoring those moments. It is about assessing whether they are becoming less dominant over time.

You are allowed to ask yourself whether you still have the emotional bandwidth to stay present while this process unfolds. Wanting rest does not make you cruel. Wanting relief does not automatically mean you should leave. It means you are human.

Staying is courageous when it is chosen freely, not when it is driven by fear.

Some people stay because they are terrified of the guilt that would come with leaving. Others stay because they cannot tolerate the idea of causing someone pain. In those cases, staying is not a choice. It is a reaction.

Courageous staying looks different. It is grounded in realism rather than obligation. It is chosen with open eyes. It includes the possibility of leaving later if conditions do not improve.

There is a difference between patience and self-deception.

Patience is staying while watching for change. Self-deception is staying while telling yourself that tomorrow will be different, without evidence to support that belief.

One of the most important questions you can ask yourself is not whether things are perfect, but whether they are alive.

Is the relationship moving, even slowly, toward something more balanced? Or does it feel frozen, looping through the same cycles with new explanations but the same outcomes?

Staying is not meant to cost you your integrity.

You do not need to stay until you are exhausted, numb, or resentful in order to prove that you tried hard enough. Effort does not require self-erasure. If staying requires you to consistently silence your values, shrink your life, or ignore your own limits, it has crossed from commitment into sacrifice.

There is nothing weak about choosing to stay when growth is possible. There is also nothing virtuous about staying when the evidence says otherwise.

Section 4: The Lie That Keeps People Stuck

There is a sentence many people repeat to themselves so often that it begins to sound like wisdom.

Maybe tomorrow will be better.

On the surface, this thought looks harmless. Even hopeful. It feels generous rather than naïve. After all, relationships do change. People grow. Bad days pass. Hard seasons end.

But in dependent dynamics, this sentence often becomes a way of postponing a decision that already feels overdue.

The problem is not hope. The problem is hope without structure.

Tomorrow only becomes different when something changes today. Without change, tomorrow is simply a continuation of yesterday with a new date attached to it. The calendar moves forward, but the pattern remains the same.

Many people mistake waiting for patience. In reality, waiting can be a form of avoidance. It allows you to delay the discomfort of choosing while quietly absorbing the cost of staying. Each day feels survivable on its own, even as the accumulation becomes heavier.

Hope becomes dangerous when it is no longer anchored to evidence.

You may tell yourself that things will improve once work calms down, once therapy starts, once the next crisis passes, once they feel more secure, once you explain yourself more clearly. These conditions sound reasonable, and sometimes they are. But when the list keeps growing, and the outcome stays the same, hope has shifted from possibility into self-protection.

This is how people stay far longer than they ever intended to.

The lie is not that tomorrow could be better. The lie is that tomorrow will be better without anything changing.

Real improvement leaves tracks.

It shows up in behavior, not just intention. It appears in how someone responds when stressed, not how they reflect when calm. It shows itself in what you are asked to carry and what you are no longer expected to manage.

When change is happening, you do not have to convince yourself of it. You feel it in your body. There is more space. Less vigilance. Fewer emergencies. The relationship begins to feel less like something you are holding together and more like something that can hold itself.

When change is not happening, the body knows that too.

You may notice chronic tension, dread, or exhaustion. You may feel a low-grade sense of resentment that you quickly suppress. You may tell yourself that you should be grateful, that things are not "that bad," that other people have it worse. These thoughts are not signs of strength. They are signs that you are negotiating with reality.

Another version of this lie sounds more responsible.

I can't leave yet.

People often say this because they believe there is a future moment when leaving will be justified. When the situation will be bad enough. Clear enough. Clean enough. They imagine that clarity arrives first, and then the decision follows.

Staying indefinitely in the hope that things will become obvious keeps you in limbo. You wait for a crisis that may never come, or for a change that has not yet shown itself. Meanwhile, the cost of staying continues to accrue quietly.

This does not mean you should rush to leave. It means you should be honest about what you are waiting for.

Ask yourself plainly: *What evidence would tell me that staying is working?* And just as importantly: *What evidence would tell me that it is not?*

If you cannot answer those questions, or if the answer keeps shifting to protect the status quo, hope has stopped being a guide and has started being a shield.

There is a difference between patience and paralysis.

Patience is active. It observes. It responds to information. It has limits.

Paralysis is passive. It delays. It waits for permission. It confuses endurance with virtue.

Staying becomes self-deception when you are no longer choosing it but defaulting into it.

The hardest part about releasing this lie is not fear of leaving. It is the grief of admitting that hoping alone has not been enough.

Section 5: When Staying Becomes Self-Harm

Many people believe that staying only becomes harmful when something extreme is happening. Abuse. Threats. Explosions. Clear violations that are easy to name and easy to justify leaving.

But harm does not always announce itself that way.

In dependent dynamics, the damage is often quiet. It accumulates slowly. There is not a single breaking point, but a slow erosion of self.

Staying becomes self-harm when the cost of remaining requires you to consistently move against your own values, limits, or sense of who you are. Not occasionally. Repeatedly.

This kind of harm does not need malice to exist. No one has to intend to hurt you. What matters is impact.

People often struggle here because they believe that if they agreed to stay, then the cost must be acceptable. They tell themselves they chose this. That they are consenting adults. That leaving would be dramatic or selfish.

But consent can be shaped by survival.

When you have spent a long time managing someone else's emotions, preventing escalation, or holding a relationship together through constant accommodation, your range of perceived options narrows. You adapt. You normalize what once would have felt intolerable. You stop asking whether something is fair and focus instead on whether it is manageable.

Over time, people begin to confuse endurance with commitment. They tell themselves that suffering proves love, that loyalty requires sacrifice, that their needs can wait indefinitely. What often goes unexamined is what is quietly being traded away in the process.

Energy. Integrity. Identity. Joy.

Staying becomes self-harm when you notice that your life is shrinking in order to preserve someone else's stability. When your days are organized around anticipating reactions. When your words are filtered to avoid fallout. When your needs feel like inconveniences rather than realities.

Compassion has crossed into self-betrayal.

Compassion is caring without abandoning yourself. It allows space for your own limits and does not require you to disappear.

Moral injury begins when care demands repeated violations of your own values or sense of self in the name of keeping the peace. When you find yourself acting in ways that do not align with who you believe you are, simply to prevent distress or conflict, something important has been crossed.

People often ask whether it is ethical to prioritize their own survival over someone else's stability. The honest answer is that it is often the only ethical choice in the long term.

You can temporarily stretch yourself during a crisis. You can carry more for a season. But living indefinitely in a posture of sacrifice corrodes the very qualities that made you capable of care in the first place.

A relationship that requires one person to slowly disappear for the other to function is not sustainable. Not for you. And ultimately, not for them either.

One of the most painful realizations people face is that staying longer does not always protect the other person. It delays growth and reinforces dependence.

Naming self-harm in this context does not mean assigning blame. It means acknowledging reality.

If staying requires you to silence your values, numb your emotions, or live in a constant state of self-suppression, it is no longer an act of love. It is an act of injury.

You do not need to wait for permission to protect yourself. You do not need to prove that things are bad enough. You are allowed to notice when the cost has become too high.

Section 6: What People Get Wrong About Leaving

One of the reasons deciding to leave feels so terrifying is that people are often operating under a set of assumptions that have never been examined. These beliefs feel self-evident, even moral. They are repeated internally until they harden into truth.

If I leave, they will fall apart.

If I leave, I am abandoning them.

If I leave, I am proving that I never really loved them.

These thoughts are powerful because they are not entirely fictional.

Leaving does matter. It creates disruption. It hurts. When someone has relied on you emotionally, practically, or psychologically, separation will destabilize them, at least initially. Anxiety may spike. Functioning may wobble. Anger or panic may surface. Your presence has been regulating for them, and its absence will be felt.

The distortion is not that they will struggle. The distortion is the leap from struggle to collapse.

Struggle is not the same thing as destruction. Discomfort is not the same thing as danger. Pain does not automatically mean harm is being done.

When you have been serving as the stabilizer in a dependent relationship, it can feel as though you are the only thing holding the system together. But influence is not the same as responsibility. Your presence affects the other person's emotional state, but that does not mean you are ethically obligated to remain indefinitely to prevent distress.

Adults are allowed to struggle. Growth often requires it. Another common misunderstanding is the belief that leaving means you are "washing your hands" of the other person. That you are declaring them no longer worthy of care or concern.

This is rarely true.

Leaving does not erase love. It changes the structure through which love is expressed. You can care deeply about someone and still decide that you cannot continue to organize your life around their needs.

Some people confuse boundaries with abandonment. Boundaries create limits. Abandonment removes care. The two are not the same, even if they feel similar to someone whose nervous system is highly sensitive to separation.

There is also a myth that leaving means you are condemning the other person to permanent dysfunction.

In reality, staying does not guarantee stability, and leaving does not guarantee collapse. What it does guarantee is change. That change may be painful. It may be messy. But it is often the first condition necessary for growth.

Another fear people carry is that leaving proves they were wrong to stay as long as they did. That it invalidates the effort they put in. They feel foolish for having helped. Their efforts naïve or misplaced. It means that the relationship reached a point where the structure no longer worked. That is not failure. It is information.

People also worry that leaving must be permanent to be legitimate. That if they leave, they must commit to never returning, never revisiting, never reconsidering.

This all-or-nothing thinking mirrors the very dynamics that made the relationship so exhausting in the first place.

Leaving can take many forms. Distance. Separation. Restructuring. Redefining roles. It does not always require erasing someone from your life. It does require honesty about what you can and cannot offer.

In addiction medicine, we understand that growth is rarely linear and that abstinence-only models do not work for everyone. Harm reduction recognizes that reducing damage and increasing capacity can be meaningful steps toward health.

The same principle applies here.

Creating space does not mean you have failed. It may mean you are finally allowing the conditions for change to exist for both of you.

The hardest part is accepting that you cannot control the outcome.

You cannot ensure that they will use the space well. You cannot guarantee that they will seek help or develop new supports. You cannot protect them from every consequence of the relationship changing.

What you can do is be honest about your limits, act with as much clarity and compassion as possible, and stop confusing care with self-sacrifice.

Leaving is nothing more than a statement about what is sustainable for you.

Section 7: Leaving as a Developmental Rupture

Most people think of leaving as an ending. A collapse. A declaration that something went wrong or that someone failed.

In reality, many relationships do not end because love disappears. They end because the structure that once held them no longer works for everyone involved.

Every relationship has a life cycle. It begins with connection, adapts through stress, and is shaped by the capacities of the people inside it. Some relationships evolve and rebalance over time. Others reach a point where growth within the existing structure becomes impossible.

This is what I mean by a developmental rupture.

A rupture is not the same as destruction. It is a break that creates the possibility for reorganization. In child development, growth often follows disruption. Old patterns fail. New ones form. Something that once worked no longer does, and the system has to adapt.

The same is true in adult relationships.

In dependent dynamics, staying often preserves the status quo. The roles remain intact. One person regulates, the other leans. Relief arrives, then resentment. The cycle continues. Nothing truly shifts because there is no pressure for the system to reorganize.

Leaving introduces that pressure.

This is why leaving feels so destabilizing. It interrupts a familiar equilibrium, even when that equilibrium is painful. The nervous system resists change before it adapts to it. Panic does not mean catastrophe is coming. It often means the old structure is being challenged.

By the time most people reach this chapter, leaving is not a first resort. It is something they have tried to avoid. They have explained. They have compromised. They have carried more than their share. They have waited for change. When leaving finally enters the picture, it is usually because every other option has been tested.

Seen this way, leaving is not a failure of love. It is an acknowledgment of reality.

A developmental rupture says: This structure cannot support growth for both of us as it is.

Another important misconception is that rupture must be permanent to be legitimate. That if you leave, you must close the door forever in order to prove resolve or strength.

This kind of all-or-nothing thinking is familiar in dependent systems. It mirrors the same emotional logic that turns boundaries into threats and distance into abandonment.

In practice, rupture can take many forms. It may involve separation or simply redefining roles. It may involve creating space that allows both people to develop capacities that could not emerge while the old structure remained intact.

Sometimes relationships do not resume. Sometimes they do, in altered and healthier forms. Sometimes they transform into something smaller but more sustainable. There is no single correct outcome.

What matters is that the rupture creates an opportunity for differentiation.

Differentiation means that each person becomes more responsible for their own emotional regulation, choices, and growth. In dependent dynamics, differentiation is often impossible without disruption. The old roles are too entrenched.

This is why staying indefinitely can paradoxically prevent growth, even when motivated by love. When rescue is always available, the nervous system never learns to tolerate distress independently. When stability is outsourced, autonomy cannot develop.

Leaving removes the scaffolding.

That does not guarantee growth. But it makes it possible.

This is also where compassion often gets misdirected. People fear that by leaving, they are abandoning someone at their most vulnerable moment. In reality, staying may be what keeps that vulnerability frozen in place.

A rupture is painful because it forces confrontation with reality. It removes shortcuts. It exposes limits. It demands adaptation.

None of that is cruel.

It is development.

Leaving, when it is done thoughtfully and without retaliation, is not an act of aggression. It is an act of honesty. It acknowledges that the relationship, as it currently exists, cannot continue without ongoing harm.

You are not required to stay in order to prove that you care.

You are allowed to let the structure change.

Section 8: The Grief No One Warns You About

One of the most confusing parts of leaving is not the decision itself. It is what comes after.

Many people expect relief. And relief often does come. The tension eases. The constant vigilance softens. The feeling of being on call begins to fade. There is more space in your day, more quiet in your body.

What people are rarely prepared for is that grief arrives alongside that relief.

This grief can feel disorienting because it does not match the story people expect to tell themselves. You may have wanted to leave. You may have known it was the right decision. And still, something inside you aches.

You are not grieving only the person.

You are grieving the version of the relationship you hoped for. The future you imagined. The effort you invested. The role you played for so long. You may even grieve the sense of being needed, even if it came at a cost.

None of this means you made the wrong choice.

Grief does not measure the quality of a decision. It measures attachment.

People often try to outrun this grief. They distract themselves. They fill the space quickly. They look for reassurance that leaving was justified. They ask friends to confirm that they did the right thing. They want the pain to resolve so they can move on.

But grief does not respond well to being rushed.

When you have been organized around someone else's needs for a long time, their absence creates a vacuum. That space can feel unsettling, even frightening. It is tempting to fill it immediately, with another relationship, another responsibility, another crisis to manage.

This is one of the most vulnerable moments in the process.

Filling the vacuum too quickly often recreates the very dynamics you just left. The nervous system reaches for familiarity, not health. Without time to recalibrate, old patterns slip into new forms.

Grief needs room.

It needs acknowledgment rather than explanation. It needs time to pass without being managed away. Allowing yourself to mourn does not mean you regret leaving. It means you are honoring what mattered.

Another layer of grief that often surprises people is guilt.

Even after leaving, many people continue to feel responsible for how the other person is doing. They check in mentally. They imagine scenarios. They worry that they caused lasting damage. These thoughts can surface unexpectedly, even months later.

This does not mean you should return. It means your nervous system is still unwinding from a long period of overfunctioning.

Concern can exist without obligation.

Care can exist without proximity.

Over time, if you allow it, grief changes shape. It becomes less sharp. Less consuming. It no longer dictates your decisions. It becomes part of your story rather than the center of it.

People often fear that if they let themselves feel this grief fully, they will collapse or be pulled back into the relationship. In reality, grief felt honestly tends to loosen its grip. What keeps people stuck is not grief, but resistance to it.

There is no timetable here.

You do not need to be "over it" to move forward. You do not need to justify your decision repeatedly. You do not need to perform closure.

You are allowed to miss someone and still know that staying was not sustainable.

You are allowed to mourn what was lost without reopening what was harmful.

Grief, in this context, is not a sign of weakness.

It is a sign that you cared deeply.

And caring deeply does not obligate you to keep suffering.

Section 9: What Actually Happens After

When people imagine leaving, they often picture two extreme outcomes. Either everything will immediately fall apart, or everything will instantly feel better. Neither is usually true.

What tends to happen is quieter and more complex.

For the person with dependent traits, the initial period after separation is often destabilizing. The routines and emotional scaffolding they relied on are gone. Anxiety may spike. Functioning may wobble. They may feel angry, abandoned, or overwhelmed. From the outside, this can look alarming, especially if you have been the one stepping in to stabilize things.

Without immediate rescue, many people begin to adapt. Not smoothly. Not all at once. But gradually. They may seek therapy. They may lean on other supports. They may struggle, regress, and then try again. The absence of a constant regulator forces the nervous system to attempt new strategies.

Growth is not guaranteed. But it becomes possible.

For the person who leaves, the early period is often marked by emotional oscillation. Relief arrives in waves. So does guilt. There may be moments of clarity followed by moments of doubt. You may worry about how the other person is doing, even when you know you cannot go back to the old structure.

This is normal.

You are grieving and reorganizing at the same time.

Many people experience what feels like the stages of grief, though not in a neat or predictable order. Sadness, anger, bargaining, numbness, acceptance. These emotions can overlap and repeat. They do not mean you are backsliding. They mean your nervous system is recalibrating.

Over time, something else begins to happen.

Your energy returns. Your thoughts feel less consumed. You notice that your days are no longer structured around anticipating someone else's needs or reactions. The background tension that once felt constant begins to fade.

You may still think about the other person. You may still care. But the concern becomes proportionate rather than consuming. It takes up space in your life rather than defining it.

One of the most consistent patterns I see clinically is that people tend to leave too late, not too early.

By the time they act, they are often exhausted, resentful, or numb. They have stayed long past the point where the relationship could realistically rebalance. They have sacrificed more than they needed to in order to prove loyalty or compassion.

Leaving too early does happen, but far less often. It is more common among people who have a low tolerance for relational discomfort or who equate challenge with danger.

If you are here, you have likely already tried.

Another reality that clinicians do not always say out loud is that no one emerges from these decisions untouched. There is no path that avoids pain entirely. Staying hurts. Leaving hurts. What matters is not eliminating pain, but choosing which pain is more honest and more sustainable.

The goal is not to erase the relationship from your life or memory. It is to stop living inside a structure that required you to disappear.

With time, most people reach a steadier place. The decision settles. The noise quiets. The constant questioning fades.

What remains is not triumph or regret, but clarity.

And clarity, unlike urgency, tends to last.

Section 10: A Hand on the Reader's Back

If you have made it to this point, you are not careless. You are not impulsive. You are not looking for an easy way out.

You are someone who has thought deeply, tried honestly, and carried more than most people ever see.

This decision does not ask you to be certain. It asks you to be truthful.

You do not need to vilify anyone in order to leave. You do not need to erase the love that existed. You do not need to prove that things were bad enough or justify yourself to an imaginary jury.

You are allowed to choose what is sustainable.

Leaving does not make you cold. Staying does not make you noble. Neither option defines your character. What matters is whether the structure of the relationship allows you to remain whole.

If you decide to stay, let it be because you see real movement, not because guilt has made the alternative feel unbearable. If you decide to go, let it be because you are protecting your integrity, not because you are fleeing discomfort.

You can care deeply about someone and still decide that you cannot continue in the same way.

You can walk away without slamming the door.

You can hold love and limits at the same time.

There may be days after this decision when you question yourself. Where you miss what was familiar. Where you worry about the other person. None of that means you were wrong. It means you are human.

You do not have to rush yourself through the aftermath. You do not have to arrive at peace immediately. Peace tends to come quietly, after you stop arguing with yourself.

If you woke up tomorrow and this relationship no longer structured your days, how would you feel after the initial grief settled?

That answer matters.

Whatever you choose, you are allowed to choose it without shame.

You are allowed to trust that you have done your best with what you knew at the time.

You are allowed to step forward into your life again.

And you do not have to do it alone.

CHAPTER 13

Healing Yourself After Suffocation

Section 1: What Healing Actually Means After Suffocation

When people imagine healing after a suffocating relationship, they often picture a dramatic emotional shift. Relief. Freedom. Lightness. A sense of being "back to normal."

That image is understandable. It is also incomplete.

Healing, in this context, is not the absence of memory or feeling. It is not forgetting the person. It is not needing to rewrite the relationship as terrible in order to justify leaving.

Healing is the return to wholeness.

Wholeness means you are no longer internally divided. You are no longer pulled in multiple directions by guilt, vigilance, responsibility, and self-suppression. Your nervous system is no longer on constant alert, anticipating the next request, the next emotional shift, the next situation that will require you to step in and stabilize.

One of the clearest signs of healing is the quieting of mental noise. There is less rehearsal. Less strategizing. Less planning for hypothetical outcomes. You are no longer spending significant portions of your day thinking about how to manage someone else's reactions, emotions, or needs.

That does not mean you never think of them.

Memories still surface. A song on the radio. A holiday. A familiar restaurant. A shared routine. These moments can carry warmth, sadness, or tenderness. These feelings are not a failure of healing. It is evidence that the relationship mattered.

What changes is what happens next.

In healing, the memory passes without mobilization. Your body does not tense. Your mind does not race. You do not feel compelled to act, reach out, fix, or revisit. The feeling moves through you rather than pulling you back into a role.

This distinction matters.

Many people fear that if they still care, still remember, still feel affection at times, then they have not healed. In reality, healing does not eliminate feeling. It restores choice.

Another common misconception is that healing should feel energizing right away. That you should feel lighter, stronger, or more confident as soon as the suffocating dynamic ends. For some people, moments of relief do appear early. But for many, healing feels quieter and more internal.

It often feels like less, not more.

Less urgency.

Less emotional noise.

Less pressure to perform or prove.

At first, that reduction can feel unsettling. When your nervous system has been organized around responsibility and vigilance for a long time, the absence of those demands can feel unfamiliar rather than immediately comforting. Some people mistake that unfamiliarity for emptiness or loss of purpose.

Healing is not about filling that space quickly. It is about allowing it to exist long enough for your system to recalibrate and for your sense of self to reemerge without being defined by obligation.

In that sense, healing is not something you force. It is something that unfolds when the conditions are right. Distance creates a vacuum. The work is not to rush to fill it, but to tolerate it without resistance.

Acceptance and self-compassion are not abstract ideals here. They are practical acts. They allow the nervous system to stand down. They allow identity to reorganize. They allow you to experience yourself without the constant pull of someone else's needs.

Healing does not announce itself dramatically. It shows up quietly, in moments where you realize you are no longer bracing. Where you are no longer negotiating with yourself. Where you are simply present in your own life.

Section 2: The Aftermath No One Prepares You For

Most people are not prepared for what happens emotionally after they create distance from a suffocating relationship.

They expect a clean arc. Decision, relief, resolution.

What usually follows is something messier and more human.

In the early phase, relief often arrives first. The tension eases. The constant sense of being "on" softens. The immediate pressure to manage, respond, or anticipate diminishes. Many people notice a subtle lightness in their body, sometimes for the first time in years.

Then, almost inevitably, something else appears.

Guilt.

Self-doubt.

Second-guessing.

You may find yourself asking questions you thought you had already answered. Was I too harsh? Did I overreact? Could I have tried longer? Did I abandon them?

These thoughts can feel alarming, especially if you believed that clarity would eliminate doubt. Many people interpret this internal questioning as evidence that they made the wrong decision.

It is not.

This oscillation is not a sign of failure. It is a predictable part of disentangling from a role-based attachment.

When you have spent a long time stabilizing someone else, your nervous system has learned that separation equals danger. Even when separation is necessary and chosen thoughtfully, the body reacts before it updates. Doubt and guilt rush in as attempts to restore familiarity.

Another layer of this phase is shame.

Some people feel embarrassed that the relationship did not work, especially if they invested heavily or defended it for a long time. Others worry about how they will be perceived by friends or family. Many struggle with the idea that they "abandoned" someone who felt vulnerable or dependent.

This shame can be particularly strong for people who pride themselves on being loyal, capable, and compassionate.

What often gets missed is this: by the time most people reach this point, they have already tried extensively. They have explained. Adjusted. Accommodated. Carried more than their share. The decision to create distance rarely comes impulsively. It comes after exhaustion.

Knowing that does not instantly erase guilt, but it often brings more internal peace than people expect.

Another common experience in this phase is misinterpreting external cues as proof of error. For example, seeing the former partner appear stable, independent, or content early on can trigger painful self-doubt. People think, maybe it was just me. Maybe I imagined the problem.

This conclusion is usually based on incomplete information.

Dependent dynamics often do not reveal themselves immediately. Early functioning does not reflect long-term patterns, and outside observation rarely captures what happens behind closed doors. When the mind selectively gathers evidence to support regret, it is engaging in a familiar strategy: trying to regain certainty.

The mind prefers regret over ambiguity.

What is actually happening in this phase is not regression. It is adjustment.

You are grieving and reorganizing at the same time. Your nervous system is learning a new orientation. That process is rarely linear. Relief and grief coexist. Confidence and doubt alternate. This does not mean you are backsliding. It means your system is recalibrating.

Understanding this phase matters because misinterpreting it can pull people back into old roles prematurely. The discomfort of uncertainty can feel so intense that returning to what is familiar seems like the fastest way to relieve it.

Healing requires tolerating this middle space without rushing to resolve it. It's often a test of your patience.

And it passes, not because you force it to, but because your system gradually learns that the absence of constant responsibility is not dangerous.

Section 3: When the Role Disappears and Identity Wobbles

In suffocating relationships, identity rarely disappears all at once. It narrows.

Over time, many people slide into a role that becomes quietly central to who they are. They become the stabilizer. The crisis manager. The emotional anchor. The one who notices first, intervenes fastest, and absorbs the fallout so things do not fall apart.

At first, this role feels meaningful. It offers purpose and coherence. You know what is expected of you. You know where to place your attention. You know how to be useful.

Eventually, it becomes exhausting.

But even when it is exhausting, the role still provides structure. It organizes your days. It tells you who you are in the relationship. It gives you a clear answer to the question, "Why am I here?"

When that role disappears, either because you leave or because the dynamic changes, the absence can feel destabilizing in ways people do not anticipate.

Many expect relief to dominate. Instead, what often arrives first is disorientation.

Your nervous system had been organized around monitoring, soothing, and responding. When that constant demand is removed, the sudden quiet can feel unfamiliar rather than calming. You may notice restlessness, a drop in motivation, or a vague sense of emptiness that is hard to name.

When people say, "I don't know who I am anymore," they are often grieving the loss of a function-based identity. They are mourning the version of themselves that was needed, relied upon, and indispensable. That identity was reinforced daily through urgency and responsibility. Its disappearance can feel like a loss of self, even when the self beneath it remains intact.

There is also a subtle hit to self-worth that can occur during this phase. Being needed can become a proxy for being valued. When the need disappears, worth can feel temporarily unmoored. This is not because your value depended on the role, but because the role had become the most consistent source of external validation.

This wobble is not pathology.

It is transition.

The mind often tries to resolve this discomfort quickly. People ask themselves whether they made a mistake. They look for reasons to reenter the role, even briefly, just to feel grounded again. They may reach out unnecessarily, offer help that was not requested, or place themselves back in familiar dynamics under the guise of kindness.

What they are often seeking is not reconnection, but orientation.

Healing requires tolerating this period without rushing to replace the role. That can feel counterintuitive, especially for people who are accustomed to functioning through action. But identity does not rebuild through immediate substitution. It rebuilds through choice.

As the nervous system recalibrates, something important begins to happen. Without the constant pull of responsibility, preferences start to surface. Desires that were muted reappear. Limits feel clearer. You may begin to notice what you enjoy, what you avoid, and what actually restores you, not because someone else needs it, but because you do.

This process is often uneven. Some days you may feel settled and present. Other days, you may feel lost or question whether you are doing enough. That fluctuation does not mean you are regressing. It means your system is learning to organize itself around internal reference points rather than external demands.

It is also common to grieve the certainty that came with the role. Even painful structures provide predictability. Letting go of that predictability can feel unsettling, even when it is necessary. This grief deserves acknowledgment rather than judgment.

What ultimately emerges is not an identity built around fixing, rescuing, or holding things together. It is an identity defined by agency.

You are no longer who you are because you are needed. You are who you are because you choose.

That shift takes time, and it is one of the most important parts of healing after suffocation.

Section 4: Guilt Is Not a Moral Verdict

After a suffocating relationship changes, guilt often becomes the loudest emotion in the room.

It rarely shows up as a single, clear feeling. More often, it arrives as a pattern. Mental checking. Replaying conversations. Imagining worst-case scenarios. Wondering how the other person is doing. Scanning for signs that you caused harm.

These thoughts can feel urgent and convincing, especially if guilt has long been the signal that tells you when to act.

Many people interpret this guilt as a moral message. They assume it means they did something wrong, that they moved too fast, that they were unkind, or that they failed to live up to their own values. The impulse is to respond to guilt by fixing it, often by reentering the dynamic in some way.

This interpretation is understandable but often incorrect.

In the context of suffocating relationships, guilt is less a verdict and more a reflex.

When you have spent a long time equating care with responsibility, your nervous system learns that stepping back is dangerous. Guilt becomes the alarm that activates whenever you stop stabilizing someone else. It is not asking you to return because returning is right. It is asking you to return because returning is familiar.

This is why guilt can intensify precisely when you are doing something healthy.

It's almost a form of withdrawal.

When a system has been organized around chronic over-responsibility, removing that responsibility creates distress. The body protests. It offers you guilt, fear, and self-doubt as tools to restore the old balance. The pull to reach out, explain yourself again, or "just check in" is often less about compassion and more about soothing your own discomfort.

Another reason guilt is so sticky is that self-blame can feel safer than reality. Believing "I should have done more" preserves the fantasy that the outcome was still under your control. Accepting that the structure was unsustainable requires confronting limits, and limits can feel frightening when you are used to being the one who holds everything together.

Guilt also tends to flatten complexity. It ignores context. It erases the effort you put in. It reduces a long, nuanced history into a single question: *What is wrong with me for needing this?*

That question is the wrong one.

A more accurate question is: *What did this role require of me, and was that requirement sustainable?*

Guilt often spikes when you stop violating yourself. When you begin to honor your own limits. When you allow someone else to experience distress without intervening. None of those actions are moral failures. They are signs that the system is changing.

The work in this phase is not to eliminate guilt. That is rarely possible or necessary. The work is to stop obeying it automatically.

You can acknowledge guilt without letting it drive your decisions.

You can say to yourself: *I feel guilty, and I am still allowed to maintain this boundary.*

You can feel concern without turning it into action.

You can tolerate the discomfort of not fixing everything.

Over time, as your nervous system updates to the new reality, guilt begins to lose its authority. It becomes quieter. Less urgent. It no longer dictates your behavior. That shift does not come from arguing with guilt or proving it wrong. It comes from repeated experience.

Each time you do not rush back to stabilize, and nothing catastrophic happens, your system learns something new.

Guilt, in this context, is not asking you to go back.

It is asking your nervous system to learn that you are allowed to stop holding someone else together and still be a good person.

That lesson takes time.

And learning it is a central part of healing after suffocation.

Section 5: The Anger You Were Not Allowed to Feel

Anger often arrives late in the healing process.

For many people coming out of suffocating relationships, anger was not an emotion they felt safe expressing. It threatened stability. It risked escalation. It raised the possibility of withdrawal, collapse, or retaliation. Over time, anger was quietly rerouted into safer channels.

It became tension.

Fatigue.

Irritability at the wrong moments.

Self-criticism.

Emotional numbing.

This was not avoidance. It was adaptation.

In dependent dynamics, anger often feels dangerous because it challenges the story that the relationship is sustainable. Acknowledging anger means acknowledging cost. It means admitting how much you tolerated, how often you bent, and how frequently your limits were crossed. For people who value loyalty and compassion, that admission can feel disloyal or cruel.

So anger gets postponed.

When distance is finally created, anger may surface unexpectedly. Not always as rage, but as a sober realization. You may notice moments of resentment, flashes of irritation, or a quiet sense of indignation about how much you carried. These feelings can be unsettling, especially if you have prided yourself on being patient or understanding.

Many people respond to this by trying to shut anger down quickly. They remind themselves that the other person did not intend harm. That they were limited. That they did the best they could. All of that may be true.

But truth does not require suppression.

Anger, in this context, is not an accusation. It is information.

It tells you where the cost was real. It points to boundaries that were violated or never allowed to exist. It highlights the gap between what you gave and what you received. Ignoring that information does not make you more compassionate. It makes you more likely to repeat the same pattern.

There is an important distinction here between anger and resentment.

Anger is a response to injury or imbalance. It is often brief and clarifying when it is allowed to be felt and understood. Resentment forms when anger is chronically suppressed or invalidated. It hardens over time and distorts perception, turning pain inward or outward in corrosive ways.

Processing anger prevents resentment.

Processing does not mean acting it out. It does not mean confrontation, punishment, or withdrawal of kindness. It means allowing yourself to name what was unfair, what hurt, and what cost you more than you realized.

You can acknowledge anger while still holding compassion for the other person's limitations. These are not mutually exclusive. Most dependent dynamics are not born from malice. They emerge from anxiety, fear, and unmet developmental needs. Recognizing that can coexist with acknowledging the impact on you.

What matters is that anger is not bypassed in the name of being "understanding."

When anger is not allowed to surface, it tends to find other exits. It can leak into new relationships. It can show up as rigidity, hyper-independence, or intolerance for closeness. It can fuel self-judgment or chronic dissatisfaction. None of these outcomes reflect healing.

Allowing anger to be felt, reflected on, and integrated restores self-respect.

A useful question in this phase is not "*Why am I angry?*" but "*What is my anger asking me to protect now?*"

Often, the answer is simple.

Your time.

Your energy.

Your autonomy.

Your right not to disappear.

Anger does not require you to harden or withdraw from the world. It does not demand that you rewrite the past or vilify the other person. It asks you to stop minimizing what you lived through.

When anger is given space without being given control, it does its job and recedes.

Section 6: How Suffocation Trains the Nervous System

One of the reasons healing after suffocation feels so confusing is that much of what needs to recover is not cognitive. It is physiological.

People often understand, intellectually, that a relationship was unsustainable. They can articulate what went wrong. They can name the patterns clearly. And yet their body continues to behave as if nothing has changed.

This is not resistance. It is conditioning.

In suffocating dynamics, the nervous system adapts to a prolonged state of unresolved threat. Not threat in the sense of overt danger, but threat in the sense of constant demand. Emotional unpredictability. The need to monitor, anticipate, and respond quickly in order to prevent escalation or collapse.

Over time, the body learns that safety depends on vigilance.

Many people live in a near-continuous state of sympathetic activation without recognizing it as stress. Hypervigilance becomes normal. Anticipatory anxiety feels like responsibility. Being "on" feels like care. The system narrows its focus toward others and away from internal cues.

Rest becomes shallow. Muscles remain tense. Breathing stays high and tight. The mind stays busy even in quiet moments. Calm, when it appears, can feel unfamiliar or even uncomfortable.

This is why insight alone rarely brings relief early on.

Understanding the dynamic does not immediately convince the nervous system that the threat has passed. The body needs repeated, lived evidence that it no longer has to perform in order to keep things stable.

One of the clearest signs that suffocation has shaped the nervous system is discomfort with quiet. When the external demands drop, many people feel restless or uneasy. They may experience a vague sense that something is wrong, even when nothing is happening. The absence of urgency can feel like emptiness.

This is not emptiness. It is the nervous system standing down from a long-held posture of readiness.

Another common sign is the persistence of urgency. Decisions feel time-sensitive even when they are not. Messages feel loaded. Pauses feel dangerous. There is a pull toward intensity, crisis, or caretaking, because those states are familiar and organizing.

People often misinterpret these sensations as evidence that they are not healing, or that they need to "do more work."

In reality, these sensations are evidence that the nervous system has not yet updated.

Physiological recovery looks less like constant calm and more like flexibility. The ability to activate when something actually requires it and to settle when it does not. Over time, sleep deepens. Startle responses soften. Muscle tension decreases. Breathing slows without conscious effort. The body begins to tolerate neutral states without anxiety.

Perhaps most importantly, people regain the capacity to be present without scanning for what might go wrong.

This process cannot be rushed.

The nervous system learns through repetition, not explanation. Each day that passes without catastrophe when you do not intervene teaches the body something new. Each boundary that holds without collapse provides corrective experience. Each moment of rest that is not interrupted by crisis retrains the system toward safety.

It is also common for people to remain in partial survival mode even after leaving. They may notice compulsive overthinking, difficulty resting without guilt, or discomfort receiving care. Some find themselves drawn to intense situations or relationships that recreate familiar patterns of urgency.

These are not personal failures. They are echoes of a system that learned connection through vigilance.

What helps most in this phase is not insight, but containment.

Predictable routines.

Consistent sleep and wake times.

Regular meals.

Days that are not constantly disrupted.

These may sound basic, but they are powerful. They reduce baseline arousal and give the nervous system something it has often lacked: reliability.

Distance, when needed, is also a physiological intervention. Continued exposure to the person or dynamic that created chronic activation can keep the system in a threat loop, even when intentions are good. Creating space is not avoidance in this context. It is how the body learns that disengagement does not equal danger.

Boundaries come next. Not as punishments or declarations, but as reliable limits. Over time, boundaries teach the nervous system that connection can exist without constant vigilance.

Therapy is most effective when it matches the phase of recovery. Early on, approaches that emphasize pacing, regulation, and meaning-making are often more helpful than intensive exploration of the past. Once the body is steadier, insight can deepen without overwhelming the system.

Body-based practices are not optional add-ons. They are often what allows everything else to work. Slow movement, breath awareness, and gentle attention to physical sensation signal safety in ways words cannot.

Healing, at this level, is not about convincing yourself that you are safe.

It is about giving your nervous system enough consistent evidence that safety is now possible.

As that evidence accumulates, the body begins to let go of its constant readiness. And when the body settles, the mind follows.

Section 7: What Actually Helps You Settle

When people are coming out of suffocation, they often want to know what to *do*.

They ask for tools. Strategies. Practices. A plan that will make the discomfort stop and signal that they are healing correctly. This impulse makes sense. Action has been how many people survived in the first place.

But settling is not about doing more. It is about doing things in the right order.

The nervous system does not respond to insight before it has safety. It responds to evidence. Healing becomes possible when your body repeatedly experiences that life is now predictable, bounded, and no longer requires constant stabilization of someone else.

Structure is not rigidity. It is containment. Regular sleep and wake times, consistent meals, predictable workdays, and repeated routines give the nervous system something it has often lacked: reliability. These rhythms lower baseline arousal and reduce the constant sense of readiness that suffocation trains into the body.

People often underestimate how powerful this is because it feels mundane. But for a system that has lived in chronic anticipation, mundanity is therapeutic.

Distance is often the next necessary ingredient.

Even when separation has already occurred, continued emotional or logistical exposure can keep the nervous system activated. Late-night messages, urgent calls, repeated updates, or ambiguous contact prevent the body from fully standing down. Reducing contact, even temporarily, is not avoidance here. It is a physiological intervention.

Distance allows your system to learn that disengagement does not equal catastrophe.

Boundaries come into play once some stability has been established. Early on, boundaries can feel activating. Guilt spikes. Self-doubt appears. That does not mean the boundary is wrong. It means the system is adjusting.

Effective boundaries in this phase are quiet and structural. They are not speeches or negotiations. They are simple limits that remain consistent over time. As boundaries hold and nothing collapses, the nervous system updates. Connection begins to feel safer because it is no longer unpredictable.

Therapy can be a powerful support, but timing and approach matter.

Insight-oriented therapy alone can backfire early if the body is still dysregulated. Endless analysis without regulation often increases rumination rather than relief. Therapy that emphasizes pacing, containment, and nervous system stabilization helps create the conditions where insight can later deepen without overwhelming the system.

Body-based practices are not optional add-ons in this phase. They are often what makes everything else effective. Slow movement, breath awareness, grounding, and gentle attention to physical sensation provide bottom-up signals of safety that the nervous system cannot receive through logic alone.

For people who are skeptical of these practices, it can help to think of them not as emotional work, but as retraining. You are teaching your body that it no longer has to brace.

What is important to emphasize is that no single intervention is sufficient on its own. People settle not because they find the perfect technique, but because their nervous system repeatedly experiences consistency across multiple areas of life.

Predictable days.

Reduced urgency.

Boundaries that hold.

Support that does not demand performance.

Over time, this consistency accumulates.

You may notice that your baseline anxiety lowers. That decisions feel less pressured. That you can tolerate quiet without scanning for what is missing. That rest no longer feels earned only after exhaustion.

These shifts are often subtle at first. People sometimes miss them because they are looking for dramatic change. But settling rarely announces itself loudly. It reveals itself in what no longer feels necessary.

You stop rehearsing conversations that may never happen.

You stop checking your phone compulsively.

You stop feeling responsible for outcomes you cannot control.

When these changes occur, they are not the result of willpower or insight alone. They are the result of your nervous system learning, through experience, that it no longer has to organize your life around someone else's instability.

That learning is cumulative.

The learning is cumulative, and once it takes hold, it becomes the foundation on which everything else in healing can be built.

Section 8: Rebuilding a Self Without Rushing It

After a long period of suffocation, there is often a powerful urge to make up for lost time.

People want to reclaim everything at once. They push themselves to feel normal again, to re-engage fully, to prove that they are fine. Some throw themselves into work. Others into new relationships, social plans, or self-improvement projects. The message underneath is often the same: *Nothing happened. I'm back.*

This impulse is understandable. It is also risky.

Rebuilding too quickly can recreate the very conditions that made the previous dynamic unsustainable. Urgency, overextension, and loss of internal reference are not healed by more activity. They are simply expressed in a new form.

Healthy rebuilding after suffocation is quieter.

In the first months, it often looks like narrowing rather than expanding. People become more selective about how they spend their time, who they see, and what they commit to. Energy is treated as a limited resource rather than something to be stretched indefinitely.

This selectivity is not withdrawal. It is discernment.

A useful way to think about rebuilding is to ask not, "*What should I do now?*" but "*What does my system tolerate without strain?*" Growth that is sustainable tends to feel grounded, even when it is uncomfortable. Growth driven by escape tends to feel pressured and brittle.

Growth expands capacity over time. It increases tolerance for feeling, ambiguity, and rest. Escape narrows experience. It keeps you busy, distracted, or emotionally unavailable in order to avoid discomfort.

The behaviors can look similar on the surface. The difference lies in the aftereffect. Growth leaves you more present. Escape leaves you more depleted.

A similar distinction applies to autonomy and isolation.

Autonomy is the ability to move toward and away from connection without fear. It restores energy. Isolation is a defensive withdrawal that reduces vulnerability but also diminishes vitality. In autonomy, time alone feels chosen. In isolation, it feels compulsory.

Independence and rigidity can also be easily confused.

Healthy independence allows interdependence. It includes the ability to ask for help, receive care, and soften without collapsing. Rigidity is independence used as armor. It is marked by control, intolerance for unpredictability, and a refusal to rely on anyone, even when it would be supportive.

Rebuilding requires learning to track these internal cues rather than relying on rules.

This is where choice becomes central.

In suffocating dynamics, identity is organized around obligation. You do what is required. You anticipate what is needed. Choice narrows because not choosing feels dangerous. Healing reintroduces choice at the nervous system level.

Early choices are often small. When to rest. How much contact to tolerate. Which invitations to decline. Whether to speak up or stay quiet. Each choice provides corrective experience. It teaches your system that you can act based on internal signals and remain safe.

Over time, repeated choice rebuilds identity.

You begin to trust your preferences. You notice what drains you and what restores you. You make decisions without immediately scanning for how they will land on someone else. This does not make you less caring. It makes you more self-directed.

It is common during this phase to feel moments of doubt. People worry that they are becoming selfish, guarded, or closed off. These concerns deserve attention, but they are not proof of wrongdoing. They often reflect the discomfort of inhabiting a self that is no longer organized around rescue.

Rebuilding is not about constructing a new persona. It is about allowing the original self, obscured by years of adaptation, to reemerge.

This process is not linear. Some days you may feel clear and grounded. Other days, you may feel uncertain or fatigued. That fluctuation is not regression. It is integration.

The measure of progress is not how much you are doing, but how you are doing it.

If your life feels more internally referenced, more regulated, and less reactive, rebuilding is happening, even if it feels slow.

And slow, in this context, is not a failure.

It is a sign that healing is allowed to take root.

Section 9: Loving Without Returning

One of the most difficult ideas for people to accept after leaving a suffocating relationship is that love does not have to disappear in order for distance to remain necessary.

Many people assume there are only two options. Either they sever emotional ties completely, or they remain available in ways that eventually pull them back into the same role. This all-or-nothing thinking mirrors the very dynamics that made the relationship exhausting in the first place.

Love and obligation are not the same thing.

You can care deeply about someone and still recognize that the structure of the relationship was not sustainable. You can feel affection, concern, or tenderness without organizing your life around preventing their distress.

Love does not require proximity. It does not require constant access. It does not require self-erasure.

What often confuses people is that in dependent dynamics, love became fused with responsibility. Caring means managing. Attachment means vigilance. Distance feels indistinguishable from harm.

Healing involves separating these concepts.

Moving on does not mean you stop thinking about the person or that memories lose their emotional charge entirely. It means that those memories no longer mobilize you. Your nervous system is no longer compelled to act, fix, or return in order to relieve discomfort. The mind may remember, but the body stays settled.

This distinction is critical.

Many people believe they have not moved on because they still feel something. In reality, the true marker of moving on is not emotional neutrality, but physiological quiet. You can remember without bracing. You can care without urgency. You can think of the relationship without being pulled back into a role.

Another source of confusion is the idea that leaving must be permanent to be legitimate. Some people feel pressure to declare that they will never reconsider, never reconnect, never allow the relationship to evolve. This rigidity is often driven by fear rather than clarity.

What matters is not permanence. What matters is structure.

Any form of reconnection, if it ever occurs, must be fundamentally different. It cannot rely on the same roles, expectations, or patterns of regulation. Without structural change, returning to contact simply reinstates the conditions that led to suffocation in the first place.

For many relationships, that level of change does not happen. Accepting this is part of maturity, not pessimism. For others, growth on both sides eventually allows for a different form of connection. This is not something you can force or plan. It is something that can only be assessed over time, through consistent behavior rather than hope.

The key test is choice.

When love exists without obligation, you have freedom. You can choose contact or distance based on capacity rather than guilt. You can say yes without resentment and no without collapse. You are not compelled by fear of consequence or moral indebtedness.

Obligation panics in the presence of choice. Love does not.

This distinction becomes clearer as healing progresses. When obligation loosens, you may notice that your feelings change shape. They become less intense, less consuming, and more integrated into your life rather than dominating it. Concern becomes proportionate. Care becomes quieter.

Some people fear that allowing love to remain will weaken their resolve. In practice, the opposite is often true. When love is no longer tied to responsibility, it loses its power to trap you.

You are allowed to hold complexity. To acknowledge that something mattered and still recognize that it could not continue in the same way. To grieve what was real without reopening what was harmful.

Loving without returning is not a contradiction.

It is a sign that you are no longer confusing care with captivity.

Section 10: Strength Redefined and the Way Forward

Many people come into healing with a familiar definition of strength.

Strength meant endurance.

Strength meant tolerating more.

Strength meant staying calm, staying capable, staying in control, even when it cost you.

In suffocating relationships, strength was measured by how much you could carry without breaking.

Healing requires a different definition.

Strength, now, is not about how much you can withstand. It is about how clearly you can recognize your limits and live within them without apology. It is the ability to remain regulated when you choose yourself. It is the capacity to let someone else be uncomfortable without rushing to intervene.

This kind of strength is quieter. It does not announce itself. It does not need to be proven.

It shows up in small, consistent ways.

You pause before responding instead of reacting.

You notice when something feels off and take it seriously.

You rest without waiting for exhaustion to justify it.

You make decisions based on capacity rather than obligation.

These choices may feel unfamiliar at first. For a long time, your life may have been organized around preventing distress, not honoring preference. When that orientation shifts, it can feel strange, even selfish.

It is not selfish.

It is coherent.

Healing does not mean becoming hard, detached, or closed. It does not require shutting down empathy or withdrawing from connection. What it asks is that you stop confusing care with sacrifice.

You are allowed to remain compassionate without being consumed.

You are allowed to love without disappearing.

You are allowed to build a life that is not organized around someone else's stability.

As healing progresses, many people notice a subtle but important change. Their life begins to feel like it belongs to them again. Time feels less urgent. Decisions feel less pressured. The constant background hum of responsibility fades.

Agency returns not as a dramatic revelation, but as a quiet knowing.

You trust yourself more.

You rely less on external validation.

You feel less compelled to explain or justify your choices.

This does not mean uncertainty disappears. It means uncertainty no longer controls you.

There will still be moments of doubt. Memories may still surface. Guilt may still whisper from time to time. These experiences do not signal failure. They are remnants of a system that once required you to be more than human.

What matters is that you no longer organize your life around those voices.

Alignment between what you feel, what you value, and how you act. Alignment between your nervous system and your choices. Alignment between love and limits.

If there is one truth to carry with you from this chapter, it is this:

> You are not failing at love or strength by needing space.
>
> Your nervous system is learning that you are allowed to exist without holding someone else together.

Healing is not about erasing the past or rushing into a new identity. It is about living from a place where your presence in the world does not require your disappearance.

That is not a small achievement.

It is the foundation for everything that comes next.

CHAPTER 14

A New Model of Caring

Section 1: Why the Old Model of Caring Was Never Sustainable

Most people who end up in suffocating relationships do not lack empathy. They lack a workable definition of care.

If you look closely at how caring operated in these relationships, there was usually an unspoken rule running the entire system: *If they're okay, I'm okay.* Their emotional state quietly became the barometer for your own safety, peace, and worth. When they were calm, you could breathe. When they were distressed, everything inside you mobilized to restore equilibrium.

This didn't start as pathology. It started as love, responsibility, and a desire to do the right thing.

Over time, however, caring became less about connection and more about relief. Calm was rewarded. Tranquility felt like success. If you could bring the relationship back to a quiet, stable place, even temporarily, it felt like a win. You learned, implicitly, that peace had to be chased and maintained, not shared.

The problem is that this model of caring optimizes for short-term calm, not long-term health.

What it rewards is the absence of distress, not the presence of growth. When things are quiet, you feel good. When tension appears, you feel compelled to act. Over time, your nervous system begins to associate caring with constant vigilance. Love becomes something you *do*, not something you inhabit.

The costs of this don't appear all at once. They accumulate slowly and quietly.

Identity narrows. Desire fades. Joy becomes conditional. Integrity erodes in small ways as you explain yourself more than you mean to, tolerate more than you should, and postpone parts of your life to keep the peace. Intimacy becomes shallow, not because you don't care, but because one person is always managing the emotional climate.

This model is especially seductive for capable, high-functioning people.

If you're smart, competent, and used to solving problems, it's easy to slip into a savior role. You know how to fix things. You know how to stay calm under pressure. You tell yourself that you can carry a little more, stretch a little further, absorb one more crisis. There's often a subtle pride in this at first. Being needed feels meaningful.

But this kind of caring has an expiration date.

Eventually, the weight exceeds your capacity. What once felt generous begins to feel obligatory. What once felt loving begins to feel suffocating. And because the system was built on relief rather than sustainability, there's no graceful way for it to adapt. It only knows how to ask for more.

This is why the phrase *"I just care too much"* is so misleading.

When people say this, they're usually not describing excess empathy. They're describing over-responsibility. Healthy caring does not cost you your sleep, your stability, or your sense of self. It does not require constant anxiety or moral pressure. When caring leaves you depleted, resentful, or chronically on edge, the problem is not that you love too deeply. It's that love was taught to you as self-sacrifice rather than self-respect.

There is also fear hiding inside that phrase. Fear of conflict. Fear of abandonment. Fear of being seen as selfish or cruel. Over-giving can feel safer than setting limits, because limits risk displeasure and distance.

Section 2: Caring vs Carrying: The Distinction That Changes Everything

One of the most important distinctions in this entire book is the difference between **caring about someone** and **carrying responsibility for someone**.

Most people understand this difference intellectually. Very few recognize it in their bodies.

Your body often knows the difference before your mind does.

Caring about someone feels open and steady. There is concern, sometimes sadness or worry, but your body remains available. Your breathing stays slow. Your shoulders stay relaxed. You can think in full sentences. You can engage, step back, and return without urgency. If nothing changes today, you may feel disappointed, but you remain intact.

Carrying responsibility for someone feels entirely different. The body tightens. The jaw clenches. The chest compresses. Thoughts speed up into contingency planning. You feel compelled to act, check, fix, remind, or intervene. Silence feels intolerable. Not doing something feels irresponsible. Relief only comes after action, and even then, it's temporary.

That tension is not love. It's your nervous system bracing to prevent a perceived catastrophe.

This is why carrying responsibility often feels more moral than caring. It feels active, self-sacrificing, and urgent. It creates the illusion that if you stay vigilant enough, you can prevent collapse. But over time, carrying does not strengthen the relationship. It weakens both people inside it.

There's an analogy that captures this clearly.

If you see a butterfly struggling to emerge from its cocoon and you cut the cocoon open to help, the butterfly doesn't survive. The struggle is not an accident. The pressure of pushing out is what forces fluid into the wings and strengthens them for flight. When you remove the struggle, you don't create ease. You create fragility.

Over-caring works the same way.

When you rush in to soothe, fix, explain, or absorb distress, you relieve pressure that is actually developmental. You're not just reducing pain. You're interrupting the process by which resilience, agency, and self-regulation form. The other person may feel calmer in the moment, but their nervous system learns something dangerous: *I cannot tolerate discomfort without intervention.*

Dignity is built by surviving one's own emotions. Agency is built by owning choices and consequences. Carrying responsibility for someone deprives them of both, even when it's done with love.

True caring stays nearby without taking over. It allows struggle without abandonment. It tolerates uncertainty without control. It communicates, *I believe you can endure this, and I don't need to disappear to prove I care.*

This is the structural difference.

Caring preserves two separate nervous systems. Carrying fuses them.

Caring allows choice. Carrying creates compulsion.

If your care is accompanied by muscle tension, racing thoughts, and a shrinking sense of freedom, your body is telling you that responsibility has crossed a line that healthy caring never requires.

Learning to feel that difference, not just understand it, is the first step in adopting a new model of care.

Section 3: Responsibility Has a Shape

One of the most destabilizing moments in shifting how you care is realizing that responsibility is not infinite. It has edges. It has limits. And when those limits are crossed, caring quietly turns into something else.

Most people were never taught this.

If you loved someone, you absorbed more of it. If they struggled, you took on extra. If they fell apart, you stepped in. The clearer your conscience felt, the more responsibility you assumed.

Healthy caring depends on assigning responsibility to the right place. When responsibility drifts upward onto the most capable, conscientious person in the room, the entire system distorts. One person becomes heavier. The other becomes lighter. Neither grows.

Clinically, I find it helpful to make this distinction explicit.

You are responsible for your words, your actions, and your choices. You are responsible for how you communicate care and how you hold your limits. You are responsible for regulating your own nervous system and for seeking help when you are overwhelmed. You are responsible for deciding how much access someone has to your time, energy, and emotional life.

You are not responsible for another adult's emotions.

You are not responsible for how someone reacts to your boundaries.

You are not responsible for preventing disappointment, anxiety, or pain.

You are not responsible for fixing someone else's life, regulating their nervous system, or ensuring they turn out okay.

This distinction often sounds harsh at first, especially to people who have been praised for being reliable, selfless, or endlessly available. But it is not a withdrawal of care. It is a correction of misplacement.

Many people confuse support with stabilization.

Support means offering help that is voluntary, proportionate, and sustainable. Stabilization means stepping in to prevent collapse. Substitution means taking over a task, role, or responsibility entirely. In suffocating dynamics, these distinctions blur. What begins as support quietly turns into stabilization and then substitution, until one person is carrying far more than they realize.

Preventing pain feels kinder than allowing struggle. Watching someone you love be distressed can feel unbearable, especially if you believe that distress signals danger. But distress is not the same thing as harm. Frustration, disappointment, anxiety, and sadness are part of being human. When you rush to eliminate them, you may be protecting yourself from discomfort more than you are protecting the other person.

Natural consequences are not punishments. They are teachers.

When people are shielded from the consequences of their behavior, they do not become safer. They become dependent. Responsibility is learned through experience, not explanation. Agency develops when someone discovers, often imperfectly, that they can tolerate the outcome of their choices.

This is where many people feel a moral conflict. They worry that stepping back means abandoning someone, or that refusing responsibility means they are being unloving. In reality, taking responsibility for what is not yours erodes dignity on both sides. You become resentful and depleted. They become less confident and less capable.

Love does not transfer ownership of outcomes.

You can care deeply, show up consistently, and still refuse responsibility for things that do not belong to you. The moment you feel panicked, compelled, or morally pressured to manage someone else's inner world or future, responsibility has crossed a line that healthy caring never requires.

Returning responsibility to its proper place does not make relationships colder. It makes them clearer.

It allows care to be offered freely rather than under duress. It allows both people to remain adults. And it creates the conditions where connection can exist without one person slowly disappearing to keep the other afloat.

Understanding that responsibility has a shape is not an act of withdrawal.

It is an act of precision.

And precision is what allows caring to become sustainable again.

Section 4: Guilt Reinterpreted in the New Model

Guilt is often the first emotion to flare when you begin to reassign responsibility.

It can feel sudden and overwhelming. A tightness in the chest. A rush of anxious thoughts. An urgent need to fix something, explain yourself again, or step back into the role you just left. Many people take this as evidence that they've done something wrong.

In the new model of caring, that interpretation usually misses the point.

Not all guilt is moral.

Healthy guilt is informational. It appears when you violate your own values—when you lie, act cruelly, or neglect a responsibility that actually belongs to you. It is specific, proportionate, and it resolves when repair is made. This kind of guilt points you back toward integrity.

Most of the guilt that follows suffocating relationships is different.

It is conditioned guilt.

Conditioned guilt develops when your nervous system learns, through repetition, that your boundaries cause distress. Each time you say no, and someone else becomes anxious, angry, or destabilized, your body records the association: *my separation causes harm.* Over time, guilt becomes the alarm that sounds whenever you stop stabilizing someone else.

That alarm is not a verdict. It is a reflex.

This is why this guilt feels urgent and physical rather than thoughtful. It does not ask, *Did I violate my values?* It commands, *Fix this now.* Acting on it brings short-term relief, which reinforces the loop. The relief feels like proof that the action was right, when in reality it simply returned the system to what it knows.

The pattern closely resembles withdrawal.

When you remove a role that once regulated both the relationship and your own nervous system, discomfort surges. Guilt, fear, and doubt rush in to restore the old equilibrium. This does not mean the change was wrong. It means your system is adjusting to a loss of familiar structure.

Understanding this changes how you respond.

Instead of asking, "*Why do I feel guilty?*" the more useful question becomes, "*What is this guilt trying to protect me from?*" Conflict? Disapproval? Someone else's discomfort? Your own fear of being seen as unkind?

When guilt appears after healthy separation, it is often evidence that responsibility has been returned to its proper place—not that you have committed a moral failure.

This is where many people get stuck. They try to eliminate guilt before moving forward. They wait to feel confident, certain, or peaceful before holding their limits. In practice, that sequence rarely works.

Guilt fades through experience, not argument.

Each time you tolerate guilt without collapsing into rescue, your nervous system learns something new: *I can withstand this feeling and nothing catastrophic happens.* Over time, the urgency softens. The signal becomes quieter. You regain the ability to choose rather than react.

This does not mean ignoring guilt altogether. It means interpreting it accurately.

If guilt is pointing you toward repair of something that is truly yours, respond to it. If guilt is attempting to pull you back into over-responsibility, let it pass without obedience.

Learning this distinction is one of the most important skills in the new model of caring.

It allows you to remain ethical without being enslaved to anxiety. It protects compassion without turning it into self-erasure. And it frees care from the reflexive need to extinguish discomfort at any cost.

Guilt, properly understood, does not tell you to go back.

Section 5: Love Without Rescue

One of the most persistent fears people carry when they stop rescuing is the belief that they are loving less.

They watch the other person struggle, become upset, or spiral, and something inside them panics. The old model taught them that love is proven by intervention. That if distress exists and they do not act, they are withholding care or becoming cold.

In the new model, this fear needs to be addressed directly.

Love and emotional relief are not the same thing.

In many suffocating relationships, love became fused with the ability to calm someone down. If the other person felt better, the relationship felt intact. If they remained distressed, it felt like failure. Over time, soothing replaced relating. Relief replaced intimacy.

This is why stopping rescue can feel like abandonment even when presence remains.

Consider what rescue actually does. When someone is overwhelmed, and you immediately rearrange your life, over-explain, apologize for feelings you didn't cause, or take responsibility for regulating their emotions, their distress drops. Yours does too. The moment feels successful. But the structure underneath remains unchanged. They learn that collapse brings connection. You learn that connection requires disappearance.

Healthy care interrupts this pattern.

It allows you to stay emotionally present without capitulating. You can acknowledge distress without extinguishing it. You can say, *I see that you're upset. I care about you.* And you can also say, *I'm not going to fix this for you or rearrange myself to make it stop.*

To someone accustomed to rescue, this can feel shocking. The distress may escalate. Accusations may appear. The narrative often becomes: "*You've changed.*" *You don't care anymore.*

This reaction is understandable. The system has lost a familiar regulator.

But what looks like withdrawal is a shift in how love is expressed.

Rescue protects comfort. Love that holds boundaries protects capacity.

When you stop rescuing, you are not withdrawing care. You are refusing to confuse collapse with closeness. You are communicating something essential: *I believe you can tolerate your feelings, and I don't need to erase myself to prove that I care.*

This kind of love feels less dramatic. It does not come with adrenaline or produce immediate relief. And because it does not activate the same urgency, it can feel quieter, even uncertain, at first.

That quiet is often misread as distance.

In reality, it is space for two whole adults to exist.

Love without rescue does not mean indifference. It means presence without control. It means staying connected without assuming responsibility for another person's emotional state. It means allowing frustration, disappointment, and anxiety to exist without turning them into emergencies.

Over time, this changes the relationship in one of two ways.

Either the other person begins to regulate themselves more effectively, discovering that they can survive their own emotions without collapse, or the limits of the relationship become clear. Both outcomes are informative.

Love that requires your disappearance is not intimacy. It is obligation disguised as attachment.

In the new model of caring, love is measured not by how quickly you relieve distress, but by whether both people remain intact over time.

Section 6: Boundaries as the Structure That Protects Love

In the old model of caring, boundaries were often treated as a threat. They were seen as something you set when you were done being generous, or when things had already gone too far. Warmth mattered more than consistency. Intent mattered more than impact.

In the new model, boundaries serve a different function.

They are not walls. They are load-bearing beams.

A boundary says, *This is what I can offer without disappearing.* It makes care predictable rather than reactive. Without boundaries, caring collapses into resentment, exhaustion, or quiet control. With boundaries, care becomes sustainable.

This is the part people often misunderstand. Boundaries are not a reduction of love. They are what allow love to remain intact over time.

When boundaries are absent, caring is driven by guilt and urgency. You give because not giving feels dangerous. You explain because silence feels cruel. You stay available because distance feels like abandonment. Over time, this kind of care leaks resentment, even when it looks polite on the surface. The nervous system knows when generosity is coerced.

Boundaries change that.

They shift care from compulsion to choice. Instead of reacting to distress, you respond from steadiness. Instead of absorbing emotions, you allow them to exist. This does not make you less kind. It makes you more honest.

Consistency matters more than warmth here.

Warmth without consistency creates confusion. It teaches people to keep pushing until they find the version of you that gives in. Consistency, even when it is uncomfortable, teaches reliability. The nervous system relaxes not because everything is pleasant, but because the rules stop changing.

Boundaries also preserve dignity.

When you hold a boundary without disappearing, you communicate respect for the other person's capacity. You are saying, *I believe you can tolerate this.* That belief is not abandonment. It is a refusal to infantilize.

In suffocating dynamics, boundaries are often avoided because they trigger guilt or escalation. But those reactions are not evidence that the boundary is wrong. They are evidence that the old structure relied on your flexibility to function. When that flexibility is removed, the system protests.

This is where people confuse boundaries with punishment.

Punitive boundaries are rigid, emotionally charged, and designed to control outcomes. Protective boundaries are clear, calm, and designed to protect capacity. The difference shows up in the body. Protective boundaries, even when firm, reduce long-term activation. Punitive boundaries maintain tension and require constant enforcement.

Healthy boundaries do not require speeches or negotiations. They do not need repeated justification. They are simple, repeatable limits that hold over time. Their power comes from reliability, not intensity.

When boundaries are consistent, resentment has less room to grow. You stop bargaining with yourself. You stop keeping score. You stop needing to explain why you are tired or overwhelmed. Care becomes cleaner because it is no longer contaminated by self-betrayal.

Boundaries also protect the relationship from future suffocation.

They prevent emotional fusion, where one person's distress automatically becomes the other person's emergency. They keep responsibility correctly assigned. They allow connection to exist without constant vigilance.

This is why boundaries are not anti-relationship.

They are pro-relationship.

They are the structure that allows love to breathe, not the mechanism that shuts it down.

When boundaries are held with steadiness rather than fear, caring no longer requires disappearance. And once that structure is in place, the relationship, and the nervous systems inside it, can finally begin to reorganize.

Section 7: When the Other Person Resists the New Model

When you shift into a healthier model of caring, the first thing that usually happens is not relief.

It is resistance.

This catches many people off guard. They expect that clearer boundaries, calmer responses, and less rescuing will immediately improve the relationship. When instead the other person becomes more distressed, angry, or accusatory, doubt rushes in. *Did I make things worse? Am I being cruel? Was the old way actually better?*

In the old model, you were doing invisible work. You functioned as a regulator, a buffer, and an emotional shock absorber. Your flexibility, vigilance, and willingness to overextend allowed the relationship to maintain a fragile equilibrium. When you step out of that role, the equilibrium collapses before a new one can form.

The other person suddenly feels emotions that were being quietly managed for them. Anxiety spikes. Insecurity surfaces. Anger appears. From their perspective, it can feel like something essential has been taken away. The story often becomes personal: *You've changed. You don't care anymore. You're selfish. You're abandoning me.*

These reactions are less about your character and more about the nervous system losing an external stabilizer.

There is also a power shift happening.

Over-caring creates dependency without naming it. When you stop rescuing, the dependency becomes visible. The other person may escalate emotionally in an attempt to pull the old dynamic back online. Crisis, accusation, or collapse can become strategies to restore regulation.

This is the moment that tests resolve.

For the person changing their model of care, this phase is risky. You are no longer receiving the relief that rescuing once provided. The guilt and alarm remain, but the payoff is gone. Without support, structure, and alternative sources of regulation, people are vulnerable to relapse—returning to rescuing, over-explaining, or collapsing back into responsibility.

This is why preparation matters.

Healthy caring is not just about pulling back. It requires a life sturdy enough to tolerate someone else's distress without falling apart. Therapy, grounding routines, meaningful work, friendships, physical activity, and purpose all matter here. They replace the regulation that once came from rescuing.

What looks like cruelty is often just refusing to cut open the cocoon.

That single decision—to stay nearby without intervening—can feel unbearable at first. But it is often the only way for real change to occur.

Over time, one of two things usually happens.

Either the other person adapts. They protest, then slowly learn to tolerate their own emotions. Responsibility begins to redistribute. The relationship reorganizes around two nervous systems instead of one.

Or the relationship reveals its limits. The distress never settles. Boundaries are continually reframed as harm. Autonomy is punished with chaos. In these cases, the old structure was not supporting growth. It was sustaining dependency.

Neither outcome is a moral failure.

Resistance does not mean you are doing something wrong. It means you are no longer doing invisible labor that kept the system artificially stable.

The work in this phase is not to convince the other person. It is to remain consistent long enough for reality to become clear.

Healthy caring does not guarantee comfort.

It guarantees truth.

And truth, even when it arrives through turbulence, is what allows the next phase of discernment to begin.

Section 8: How to Know Whether a Relationship Can Evolve

Once the initial resistance settles, a quieter and more uncomfortable question emerges.

Can this relationship actually adapt to a healthier model of caring?

This question cannot be answered by intention, insight, or promises alone. Many people stay stuck because they keep listening to what is said rather than watching what happens. In the new model, discernment is behavioral and longitudinal, not emotional or episodic.

A relationship that can evolve will protest change, but it will not collapse under it.

Distress may appear when boundaries are first introduced. There may be frustration, sadness, or fear. What matters is not the presence of these emotions, but what happens next. Over time, distress begins to soften rather than escalate. The other person starts to self-soothe, even imperfectly. Emotional spikes shorten. Recovery happens without coercion.

Curiosity replaces accusation.

Instead of character attacks, you begin to hear questions. *Why does this feel so hard for me? What am I reacting to? What do I need to work on?* Boundaries may still be tested, but they are eventually respected. Responsibility begins to redistribute in small, uneven ways that nevertheless move in the right direction.

Your body is an important data point here.

In relationships that can adapt, your nervous system settles over weeks, not just hours. You feel clearer rather than more confused. Resentment decreases rather than goes underground. Love becomes quieter but more stable. There is less drama and more consistency.

By contrast, relationships that cannot adapt reveal themselves just as clearly.

Distress escalates without limit whenever a boundary is set. Anger turns into global judgments about your character. Boundaries are reframed as abuse, abandonment, or betrayal. There is no movement toward self-regulation, only increased demand.

Compliance is rewarded with calm. Autonomy is punished with chaos.

This pattern matters.

If the only way to restore peace is by shrinking yourself, the relationship is not reorganizing. It is reverting. Over time, you may notice that you feel progressively smaller, more anxious, or morally confused. You begin questioning values you once held firmly. You are pressured, subtly or overtly, to abandon supports, routines, or parts of your life to keep things stable.

These are not signs that you are failing at care.

They are signs that the relationship requires over-functioning to survive.

A useful question in this phase is simple but sobering: *Does this relationship tolerate two separate nervous systems, or does it require one person to collapse for the other to feel safe?*

Relationships that can evolve will eventually reorganize around mutual responsibility. They may resist change, but they adapt. Relationships that cannot will escalate until someone gives in or leaves.

Healthy caring does not destroy relationships.

It reveals them.

This is one of the hardest truths for people to accept, because it removes the fantasy that effort alone can fix structural incompatibility. You cannot love a relationship into health if it is built on dependency. You can only stop propping it up and see what remains.

Discernment is not withdrawal. It is honesty.

It allows you to stop asking, *How much more can I tolerate?* and start asking, *What is this relationship capable of becoming?*

That shift—from endurance to evaluation—is not cold.

It is the final act of respect you can offer both yourself and the relationship.

Section 9: Preventing the Quiet Return to Rescue

One of the most destabilizing moments for people who have rebuilt their model of caring is the realization that the pull to rescue never disappears completely.

It simply becomes quieter.

Most people expect relapse into over-caring to announce itself dramatically. They imagine a big mistake, a clear boundary violation, a conscious decision to "go back." In reality, regression almost never starts with behavior. It starts in the nervous system.

By the time behavior changes, the system has already shifted.

The earliest warning signs are bodily, not moral.

Urgency returns first. You feel a sudden pressure to act now, respond now, intervene now, even though nothing objectively urgent has happened. Your body tightens. Your jaw clenches. Your shoulders rise. Sleep becomes lighter. Thinking narrows. Instead of holding multiple perspectives, your mind loops around one person's mood, reaction, or outcome.

You begin rehearsing conversations again.

Guilt changes its tone. Instead of asking reflective questions like, *Did I violate my values?*, guilt becomes directive. It issues commands: *Do something. Fix this. Don't let this stand.* The discomfort feels intolerable, and action promises relief.

And relief usually comes.

That relief is the tell.

When stepping in immediately calms your body, that's not evidence you did the right thing. It's evidence that you regulated yourself by resuming a familiar role. The nervous system recognizes the old pattern and rewards it, even if the long-term cost remains the same.

Boundary erosion rarely sounds dangerous. It sounds reasonable.

Just this once.

They're really struggling.

I can handle it now.

It's different this time.

These thoughts are not decisions. They are rationalizations driven by activation.

At the same time, self-neglect creeps in quietly. Plans get canceled. Movement drops off. You disengage from grounding people. Your world narrows again, often so subtly that you don't notice until resentment returns.

That resentment is another early signal.

Resentment doesn't mean you're being asked for too much in the moment. It means responsibility has already started shifting back onto you without consent.

The most important insight here is this: relapse into rescue is not a failure of insight or character. It's a physiological reflex. Your nervous system learned, over time, that over-functioning reduced danger. When stress rises, it reaches for what once worked.

Catching this early requires a different question than most people ask.

Instead of asking, *Am I being a good person?*, ask: *Am I acting from steadiness and choice, or from pressure and relief-seeking?*

Growth does not mean you will never feel the urge to rescue again. It means you notice it sooner. You pause longer. You let the discomfort exist without immediately converting it into action.

The goal is not perfection.

The goal is interruption.

Each time you tolerate the urge without acting, the nervous system updates. Each time you choose steadiness over urgency, the old structure weakens a little more. Over time, the pull loses intensity. The pauses lengthen. Choice returns.

Healthy caring is not something you master once.

It is something you maintain by listening to your body before you listen to your justifications.

When care begins to feel tight, pressured, or compulsory, that's not a moral crisis. It's a signal. And signals are meant to be interpreted, not obeyed.

Staying attentive here is not vigilance.

It's self-respect practiced quietly, before the old scaffolding has a chance to rebuild itself.

Section 10: The Rule You Carry Forward

If this book has done its job, you are not leaving with a list of techniques.

You are leaving with a different internal posture.

Earlier chapters helped you name what was happening, tolerate the grief of change, and repair the parts of yourself that were narrowed by suffocation. This final section is about what you take with you into the rest of your life, quietly, without fanfare.

Because the goal was never to make you less caring.

It was to make your care accurate.

Most people are taught that care is proven through urgency, sacrifice, and emotional availability at all costs. That model rewards collapse and confuses intensity with love. It feels virtuous. It feels familiar. And it quietly drains the people who practice it.

The new model is simpler, but not easier at first.

It asks one primary question, again and again:

Does my care preserve dignity and capacity, for both of us?

When care is healthy, it feels steady. It does not require adrenaline. It does not shrink your life. It does not ask you to manage outcomes you cannot control. It allows disappointment without panic. It allows love without erasure.

This does not mean you will stop feeling guilt, concern, or sadness. It means those feelings no longer dictate your behavior automatically. They become information, not commands.

You will still care deeply. You will still feel pulled sometimes. You may even feel moments of doubt when you choose not to rescue, and someone else is unhappy. That does not mean you are doing something wrong.

It means you are no longer confusing responsibility with love.

The most reliable guide forward is not moral reasoning. It is your nervous system.

When care tightens your body, narrows your thinking, and demands immediate action for relief, responsibility has slipped out of alignment.

When care allows you to breathe, pause, and choose without fear of collapse, you are on solid ground.

This rule applies everywhere.

In romantic relationships, it will draw you toward partners who can tolerate their own emotions without demanding that you absorb them. Love will feel quieter, steadier, and more adult.

In parenting, it will allow you to let your children struggle without abandoning them, building resilience instead of dependence.

In work and leadership, it will free you from carrying other people's stress, allowing accountability and growth to live where they belong.

In family relationships, it will let you remain connected without becoming consumed.

You do not need to announce this shift. You do not need to explain it perfectly. You do not need to convince anyone else that your care is still real.

Care that is healthy does not require witnesses.

If there is one sentence worth carrying forward, let it be this:

If my care requires me to become anxious, urgent, or smaller, I have crossed from loving into carrying.

Section 11: After the Book Ends

When a book like this ends, many readers feel an unexpected disorientation.

Not because the ideas are unclear, but because the structure that helped hold them steady is about to disappear. For weeks or months, the pages gave language to things they felt but could not name. The chapters organized their confusion. The clarity felt containing.

Then the book closes.

Real life resumes without chapter headings.

This section exists to name that moment.

Nothing dramatic is supposed to happen now.

There is no final insight you are missing. No emotional arrival, you are supposed to reach. No version of yourself you need to become overnight in order to "prove" that this work landed.

Integration is quieter than understanding.

What usually happens next is uneven. Some days you will feel clear and solid. Other days you will notice old pulls return briefly. You may second-guess decisions you already made. You may feel tenderness toward people you could not stay close to. You may feel pride and grief at the same time.

None of this means you misunderstood the work.

It means you are living it.

The model you've learned does not ask you to stay vigilant or hyper-aware. It asks you to notice early and respond gently. To trust your body before your explanations. To pause when urgency shows up and ask whether the weight you're feeling is actually yours.

Caring accurately is not loud.

It does not require constant monitoring. It does not require you to stay on guard against becoming "too much" or "not enough." It becomes part of how you move through the world, the way you breathe, the way you choose.

If you ever feel unsure, return to the simplest test:

Does this version of care allow me to remain steady, present, and intact?

If yes, you're aligned.

If no, something has slipped into carrying again.

You don't need to fix that immediately. You don't need to judge yourself for it. You simply adjust.

That is what healthy systems do.

This book does not ask you to become colder, harder, or less compassionate. It asks you to become more precise. To care in ways that preserve dignity, autonomy, and life force, including your own.

If you carry one final reassurance with you, let it be this:

You are not late.

You are not broken.

You did not miss your chance to do this differently.

You are learning how to care without disappearing.

And that learning does not end when the book does.

It continues quietly, in moments where you pause instead of rush, choose instead of collapse, and remain whole while you love.

That is the work.

And you already know how to do it.

Section 12: The Line You Don't Cross Again

There is one line you do not cross again.

It is not dramatic. It is not announced. It does not require confrontation or explanation.

It is the moment you notice yourself getting smaller in order to keep someone else calm.

That is the line.

You may still care deeply. You may still feel tenderness, history, responsibility, or love. None of that disappears. What disappears is the belief that your disappearance is required.

You do not trade your sleep for someone else's comfort anymore.

You do not trade your clarity for someone else's relief.

You do not trade your nervous system for someone else's stability.

That is not withdrawal. That is accuracy.

From here on, care flows through you, not out of you.

You remain present without bracing.

Available without being consumed.

Kind without being erased.

And when guilt appears, as it sometimes will, you recognize it for what it is. Not a verdict. Not a command. Just an old reflex checking to see if the old role is still occupied.

It isn't.

You are allowed to let other adults feel their feelings.

You are allowed to let discomfort exist without fixing it.

You are allowed to be loved without being needed.

This is not a philosophy. It is a boundary inside your body.

Once you feel it, you won't lose it.

And even if you drift back for a moment, even if old instincts flicker, you will recognize the cost faster. You will return sooner. You will stay longer on your own side of the line.

That is how change lasts.

Not through force.

Not through vigilance.

Through remembering where you end.

Care that costs you your wholeness is no longer care.

You know that now.

And you don't cross that line again.

CONCLUSION

Coming Back to Care Without Losing Yourself

If you have reached this point in the book, something meaningful has already shifted.

You may not yet have made a change in your relationships or day-to-day circumstances. But hopefully, you are changing how you listen to yourself and how seriously you take what your body and mind have been trying to communicate for a long time.

You may still feel conflicted. You may still care deeply about someone whose presence in your life has required more from you than you are able to give. You may still feel unsure about what comes next. None of this means you have missed the point of the book. In many cases, it means the work is landing exactly where it should.

Clarity rarely arrives all at once with quick, easy certainty. More often, it arrives as a slow internal shift in orientation. A quiet but firm recognition that something you once carried without question may not belong entirely to you. A growing discomfort with the explanations that once kept you going. A subtle refusal, sometimes barely conscious, to keep disappearing in the name of care.

This book was never meant to rush you toward a decision. It was meant to slow you down enough to see the impact your efforts to love, support, endure, and stabilize are having on you. It was meant to draw your attention to the slow drift of responsibility and to help you recognize how often goodness has been measured by sacrifice rather than sustainability.

At the center of this work is one distinction.

Care versus carrying.

Once you truly understand this distinction, it becomes difficult to ignore. You begin to notice it not only in your thoughts, but in your body. In the tightening that precedes a reflexive yes. In the guilt that rises when you imagine resting. In the urgency that masquerades as concern. In the relief that follows rescue, and the resentment that slowly follows that relief.

None of these sensations mean you are unkind, selfish, or incapable of love. They mean your nervous system has learned to equate goodness with over-responsibility, and connection with vigilance.

That learning did not come from nowhere.

Many people learned it early, in environments where stability depended on someone staying alert, compliant, or emotionally available at all times. Others learned it later, in relationships where distress escalated quickly, and someone had to absorb it to keep things from falling apart. Some learned it because they were capable, intelligent, and reliable, and the world quietly rewarded them for carrying more than their share.

No matter how you learned to carry too much, I hope you now know that you no longer need to organize your life around others.

Healthy care does not require collapse. It does not require urgency. It does not require you to manage outcomes that are not yours. It does not require you to remain anxious in order to stay connected. And it does not require you to sacrifice your sleep, your stability, or your sense of self to prove your love.

Healthy care is steadier than that.

It allows concern without control. Presence without panic. Love without fusion. It preserves dignity on both sides by keeping responsibility accurately assigned. It tolerates discomfort without rushing to extinguish it. And most importantly, it leaves you intact.

If you are honest with yourself, you may already sense where care has crossed into carrying in your life. You may feel it when you imagine doing less, saying no, or stepping back. You may feel it when guilt arises, not because you have done something wrong, but because you are considering doing something different. You may feel it when calm feels unfamiliar, or when the absence of crisis leaves you oddly unsettled.

Those reactions are not moral verdicts. They are conditioned responses. They reflect how long your nervous system has been trained to stay alert in order to keep others stable or safe. When you stop performing that role, the system protests. Not because danger is present, but because familiarity has been disrupted.

This is one of the hardest parts of the work to accept.

When you change how you care, things often feel worse before they feel better. Not because the change is harmful, but because it exposes how much invisible labor you were doing. When you stop over-functioning, systems that relied on it wobble. People who you buffered from their own distress may feel it more acutely. Relationships that were stabilized by your vigilance may protest the loss of it.

This is where many people doubt themselves.

They interpret escalation as evidence that they are causing harm. They mistake discomfort for cruelty. They assume that if someone else is upset, they must be responsible. So they step back into old roles, not because those roles were healthy, but because they were familiar and temporarily relieving.

Growth requires a different tolerance.

It requires tolerating guilt without obeying it. Tolerating uncertainty without rushing to resolve it. Tolerating other people's feelings without absorbing them. And tolerating your own discomfort long enough for your nervous system to learn that nothing catastrophic happens when you stop carrying what was never yours.

You can learn where your responsibility ends and another person's begins. What healthy, balanced love can and cannot do. About the limits of your control, and the strength that exists on the other side of releasing it.

Some relationships can adapt to this shift. When they do, care becomes quieter and more reciprocal. There is less intensity, but more trust. Less urgency, but more respect. Two people remain present without one person having to disappear. Conflict may still exist, but it is no longer managed through collapse or rescue.

Other relationships cannot adapt.

They require one person to carry the emotional weight for both. They rely on guilt, fear, or escalation to maintain closeness. In those cases, clarity does not always lead to reconciliation. Sometimes it leads to distance. Sometimes it leads to grief. Sometimes it leads to endings that are painful, even when they are necessary.

Those outcomes are not failures.

A relationship that cannot tolerate two separate nervous systems is not healthy. It is sustained by your over-functioning. Letting that structure collapse may feel devastating, but it is also necessary and honest. And honesty, while painful, is less corrosive than living indefinitely in a role that requires self-erasure.

Grief deserves a place here.

You may grieve the person you hoped they would become. You may grieve the version of yourself that stayed longer than was sustainable. You may grieve the time, energy, or opportunity that was quietly sacrificed. You may even grieve the sense of purpose that came from being needed.

Grief does not mean the work failed. It means you cared deeply. The goal was never to remove feeling. It was to remove compulsion.

As you move forward, you may notice subtle but meaningful changes. Your decisions may slow down. Your responses may feel less urgent. You may find yourself pausing instead of fixing, listening instead of managing, choosing instead of collapsing. You may feel less dramatic relief, but more stable ease. Less intensity, but more clarity.

This is what care feels like when it is no longer fused with responsibility.

You will not do this perfectly. No one does. Old patterns resurface under stress, fatigue, or emotional pull. Growth does not mean the urge to rescue disappears forever. It means you recognize it sooner. You notice it in your body. You pause before acting. You ask whether your response is coming from steadiness or pressure.

That pause changes everything.

It gives you back agency. It gives others back dignity. And it gives relationships the chance to reorganize around reciprocal care rather than fear and dependency.

If there is one internal rule worth carrying forward, it is this:

> If my care requires me to become anxious, urgent, or smaller, responsibility has drifted.

You are allowed to care without carrying.

You are allowed to love without rescuing.

You are allowed to step back without disappearing.

You are allowed to remain whole.

Care rooted in clarity is stronger than care rooted in fear.

You do not need to decide everything now. You do not need to act immediately. You do not need to resolve every relationship or emotion before closing this book.

You only need to continue listening to yourself with the same seriousness and respect you have long extended to others.

That is where care begins again.

ACKNOWLEDGMENTS

Writing a book is one of the most solitary and most collaborative things a person can do. This one would not exist without the people who held the space while I filled it.

To my wife. Your strength, independence, and trust are the foundation everything else is built on. You have never made your support conditional, and you have always made space rather than demanded it. This book is, in many ways, a reflection of what a healthy relationship actually looks like. Thank you for being mine.

To my children. You are the reason this work matters beyond the clinical. I hope this book reaches you one day and helps you move through your relationships with awareness, integrity, and the confidence to love without losing yourselves.

To my parents and brothers. Thank you for believing in me on the days I questioned myself. Your faith carried me further than you know.

To everyone at Mindful Care. What we have built together is proof that mental health care can be both excellent and accessible. I am grateful every day to do this work alongside you.

To the team at Manhattan Book Group. Thank you for believing this message deserved a wider audience.

To Howie Mandel. Thank you for lending your voice, your story, and your platform to open this book. Your willingness to speak honestly about mental health has helped more people than you know, and your foreword set exactly the right tone for everything that follows.

To Dr. Pardeshi, my greatest mentor in psychiatry. You showed me what it means to be a clinician of real depth and integrity, and your influence runs through my practice every day.

To Dr. Taylor, my greatest mentor in research and academia. You taught me how to ask better questions and how to hold intellectual rigor alongside human compassion. That combination has defined how I think about this field.

To my attending physicians who trained me in psychiatry: Dr. Nichols, Dr. Taglienti, Dr. Donoghue, Dr. Delgado, Dr. Fast, Dr. Mohsin, Dr. Farooq, Dr. Chacko, Dr. Lima, Dr. Azizi, Dr. Fink, Dr. Surdhar, and Dr. Chen. You gave me the foundation. Everything I have built since stands on what you gave me in those early years.

To my business mentors and professors at the University of Chicago Booth School of Business, and especially to Professor Waverly Deutsch. You taught me that building something meaningful requires the same discipline and rigor as clinical work. That lesson shaped how I built Mindful Care, and it shaped how I approached this book.

To Professor Yaron Peleg, who refused to accept anything less than my best and taught me early that real effort is not something you approximate. That standard followed me into everything I have built.

To my patients. You are the reason this book exists. Every person who sat across from me and trusted me with their most exhausting, confusing, and painful dynamics taught me something that no textbook could. Your courage to look honestly at what was happening, and to ask for something different, shaped every page of this work. Thank you for letting me be part of that.

To Dougie. Thank you for believing in this project, its mission, and its purpose.

RESOURCES

If this book has raised questions or concerns about your own mental health or relationships, you do not have to navigate that alone. The following organizations offer support, information, and pathways to professional care.

Mental Health & Crisis Support

988 Suicide & Crisis Lifeline Call or text 988 (US). Free, confidential support 24/7 for people in distress.

Crisis Text Line Text HOME to 741741. Free crisis counseling by text, 24/7.

NAMI Helpline National Alliance on Mental Illness. Call 1-800-950-6264 or text "NAMI" to 741741.

SAMHSA National Helpline 1-800-662-4357. Free, confidential treatment referrals and information, 24/7.

Codependency & Relationship Support

Co-Dependents Anonymous (CoDA) coda.org. A 12-step fellowship for people seeking healthy relationships.

Al-Anon Family Groups al-anon.org. Support for families and friends of people with alcohol use disorder.

Nar-Anon Family Groups nar-anon.org. Support for those affected by a loved one's drug addiction.

Eating Disorder Support

National Alliance for Eating Disorders allianceforeatingdisorders.com. Helpline: 1-866-662-1235.

Finding a Therapist

Psychology Today Therapist Finder psychologytoday.com/us/therapists

Open Path Collective openpathcollective.org. Affordable therapy for those without adequate insurance coverage.

SAMHSA Treatment Locator findtreatment.gov. Find mental health and substance use treatment near you.

Urgent Mental Health Care

Mindful Care mindful.care. Same-day mental health urgent care across New York, New Jersey, and Connecticut, with telehealth available.

If you are unsure where to start, speaking with your primary care physician is always a reasonable first step. You deserve support that is both accessible and effective.

CONNECT WITH THE AUTHOR

If this book resonated with you, Dr. Aldad is available for keynote speaking, workshops, and media engagements on codependency, mental health leadership, and building healthier relationships in high-stakes environments.

To learn more about upcoming events, speaking availability, and additional resources, visit:

www.tamiraldadmd.com

You can also learn more about Mindful Care at mindful.care.

www.ingramcontent.com/pod-product-compliance
Lightning Source LLC
LaVergne TN
LVHW100725061126
851857LV00011B/400
* 9 7 8 1 9 7 0 8 4 4 9 6 2 *